IMF
NOT BOUND

Locked Up, But Not Locked Down!

EDITH M. PAGE, RN

Be encourged!
God is still on the Throne.

Edith M Page RN
01-26-2019

IMPRISONED, BUT NOT BOUND

Copyright © November 2018

Edith M. Page, RN

ISBN Number: 978-0-692-19457-7

Cover Design © Morris Publishing

Printed by

Morris Publishing®

Kearney, NE 68847

1-800-650-7888

TABLE OF CONTENT

FOREWORD
BISHOP DALE C. BRONNER

Life is not always fair, but God is always good! We often wonder whether the person makes the journey or the journey makes the person. As I have pondered this issue myself, I've come to the conclusion that they are clearly connected. The journey introduces the person to himself/herself. We don't honestly know what we can handle until we have to handle it. When faced with difficult situations and choices, we don't realize that we can survive until we have no alternative.

Life has many twists and turns. There are things that happen over the course of life that we would never have imagined would happen to us. But when you are an overcomer, you learn to transcend, adapt, adjust to survive and grow.

In this book, you'll see the arduous journey that Edith Page had to take in order to survive, transcend, adapt, change and grow. This is a fascinating account of being broken, then ultimately used for God's glory. I rejoice in knowing that Edith didn't allow what she went through to rob her of the good qualities that God put in her. She used imprisonment as an opportunity to draw closer to God, to learn Him in dimensions she had never known Him, to serve others, to grow in her personal discipline, and to be a victor instead of a victim.

In prison you see a full gamut of humanity—nice people, mean people, talented people, lazy people, nurturing people, selfish people, encouraging people and jealous people. People are used to test our Christian character. They help us to develop. They give us good reason to pray. They help to unveil our purpose of ministering to and serving others.

May you be inspired by the story you are about to read. May it remind you to never give up but persevere through your troubles.   All is well in the end. If all is not well, it's not the end. What is for you is for you!

Bishop Dale C. Bronner, D. Min.

Founder/Senior Pastor

Word of Faith Family Worship Cathedral

www.woffamily.org

This is the story of my journey through prison and back home.

INTRODUCTION

IMPRISONED, BUT NOT BOUND

I had been a professional registered nurse for almost thirty years, with a passion to serve people with disabilities, the mentally challenged and elderly individuals. I had been a business owner for almost twenty years. I paid my dues as I climbed the ladder of success and now to find myself being charged with the ridiculous allegation of false imprisonment, abuse to a disabled adult and operation of an unlicensed personal care home seemed unreal. I was in shock, hurt, and now angry that I've been sentenced to ten years, three to serve in prison! How in God's name has this all happened, and so fast? I felt railroaded and sold out by my own attorneys. As a business owner I'm guilty for something my employees did; really? Multiple thousands of dollars spent and I'm going to prison?

This horrible incident was meant to destroy me, but God.....

On April 12, 2016, I was sentenced by Judge Susan B. Harris to serve ten years. It was unbelievable to everyone who knew me, the outstanding work I've done and the amazing transformation that I've made in the lives of so many people. I've been a giver all my life. I was in disbelief, afraid and very confused.

Although I was bound for prison, I was not bound in prison. While serving my time, I met some of the most educated, kind and gifted people my path had never crossed. In addition, there were inmates whose families and friends abandoned them. Thankfully, I was not one of them. My family and friends were more supportive than ever. In fact, my family flew from as far as Los Angeles checking on and caring for me and the business constantly. They all assured me that I was locked up, but not locked out. They made sure I had the things I

needed to survive.

I served a one-year sentence in prison(s) and one year in a transitional center. I read the bible almost daily and realized God had a reason and a purpose for my being there. At the time, I didn't realize it, but through this period of time, I've come to realize that God was and still is in control. Nothing can happen except God allows it to be. During my sentence, I enhanced my skills as a teacher, preacher, friend and a more mindful person. This enhancement happened as a result of the time I served. In prison, I learned "what God has for you is for you." Nothing and no one can touch that.

Carrie Underwood, a seven - time Grammy-Award winner and a multiplatinum-selling entertainer was in a terrible car accident which left her with stitches on her face and in shock over how she looked. As a result of her accident, she said in her book, "A good life doesn't mean having no road blocks, it means going for what you want in spite of them." That is what God wanted me to see while in prison.

Yes, I was in prison, but being locked up did not stop me from believing in God, reading my bible, learning more about the word and finding out my divine destiny. I begin to journal on a daily basis the things that took place. My journaling helped me to keep my focus. In fact, I feel now, prison gave me more time to study the bible and while there, God was directing my path and showing me what I needed to do in the future.

I want to take this opportunity to thank my mother for teaching me to love and trust in God all my life. Without the Word in prison, I would not have made it. Nor would I have had so many opportunities. A mom's wisdom is so powerful! I love you mom.

This is what God has given me to say to you. I hope you enjoy the read. God is giving me an opportunity to do many things and I look forward to the challenge.

That's my baby.

DEDICATIONS

Dedication To My Son, Travis Keith McClendon

November 22, 1979 – July 27, 2018

This book is dedicated to my son, Travis Keith McClendon who passed away during the time I was in the transitional center. Although you are gone, you will never be forgotten. I miss you tremendously. My only regret is that I feel we didn't have enough time together and though we cannot reverse time, I look forward to seeing you again in heaven. You were so special to me and I'm sorry your time, our time, was shortened by the disease of cancer. I know you would have been proud to see this book. All I can do now is pick up the pieces and move forward. You were a gem in your own way and for that, I'm thankful to God who created you to be the person that you were. A mother's love never dies and you will always be in my memory. I Love you forever and a day! MOM.

Dedication To Ka'Laybria Meshell Turner

Travis's Only Child

This book is also being dedicated to **Ka'Laybria Meshell Turner**, Travis's only child and my one and only granddaughter. I pray that the few memories of your dad you have had will be cherished forever.

Let our experiences, the good, the bad and the ugly be used as a catalyst to fuel your future in your growth and development in Christ. I'm thankful that your mother, Juanita, has done a wonderful job in raising you to the best of her ability and your future will be brighter than your past. Please know that you have always been and will continue to be loved, cherished and cared for. I will be available to you as long as I have breath in this body. God bless you in all your endeavors. My prayer for your future is that you will allow God to lead and guide you all the days of your life according to Psalms 32:8. I Love you forever and a day, Grandma.

IMPRISONED,

BUT NOT BOUND

CHAPTER 1

MY INTRODUCTION TO PRISON: HOW DID I END UP HERE?

After spending thousands of dollars for about a year of this process of court proceedings, **April 12, 2016**, I was in court with my new high-powered super lawyer, Richard Rice, with motions he had written to present to Judge Susan B. Harris. This was the day that I was scheduled to "turn myself in" to Cobb County.   We arrived at 8:30 a.m. into Judge Harris's court room and she made us wait until almost 4:40 p.m. before she would hear the motions.

This attorney made a convincing argument with the four motions he presented. However, in my opinion Judge Harris had already made up her mind to send me to prison. After he presented the four motions, she replied "motion denied, motion denied, motion denied, motion denied. Bailiff, take her into custody." That was the last I saw of this attorney who had been paid $40,000, about 72 hours ago, thanks to one of my rich friends.

In Marietta Cobb County Detention Center, where the bailiff was polite, I was taken downstairs to change into an orange jumpsuit which I refused to put on. I told the bailiff, "I'm not staying here; my attorney will be coming to get me out of here shortly," or so I thought. The bailiff allowed me to anxiously sit and wait.

Many hours later, when I realized I was going to be processed, I changed into the jump suit and sat in a cold room waiting, just waiting. Then I fell asleep. I was awakened and walked to a pod and further into a two person cell.

Once there, I met another female waiting to go to prison. I had no idea if it would be hours, days or weeks. No one told me anything. When I saw phones on the wall, I requested to use one of them. Another inmate told me how to use the phone. It wasn't like you just picked it up and dialed out; there was a method to this madness. I had to get a proper dial out line, have money on the books, (my caller had to put money on the phone) or the caller had to accept a collect call, before I could begin to make phone calls.

My first call was to my younger sister, Cynthia, letting her know where I was and requesting her to call our mom and the rest of the family to let them know as well. My next call was to Dedric, my Godson, power of attorney and the only person I knew that could handle my business while I was away.

He was actually the only one in court with me when I was taken into custody. (Unlike during the hearing where 43 people showed up to speak in my behalf.)

I knew there was a possibility of my going to prison, but I was really hoping it didn't happen because I had my new "super lawyer." (I called him my super lawyer because he was on the legal team of our former president Bill Clinton and the Monica Lewinski case). I'd given Dedric my car keys, purse and instructions on what to do from here, just before I was taken away from the court room.

My next call was to one of my strong Spiritual friends. I called prophetess Iantha Taylor to request a good bible, and of course I was calling my attorney's office trying to find out what was next.

While incarcerated at the Marietta Cobb County Adult Detention center, I prayed and kept to myself. I sat looking at other females play cards, watch TV and sleep. It didn't take long to learn the routine. The jail routine consisted of;

- **Count**: You stood outside your cell door for a prisoner census count of heads.

- **Meals:** When they hollered chow, you got in line near the exit door where there was a slot that your food tray was slid into you. Then you walked to a bench seat style table to sit and eat your food. I hesitate to call this food. It was more like slop.

My first breakfast was dry cereal or oatmeal that was totally inedible, a carton of milk, apple sauce and something that was supposed to resemble a biscuit.

For lunch, I was served bologna and cheese or peanut butter on bread, an orange and a piece of dried cake that looked like it came from my easy bake oven I remembered having as a child. Dinner looked like peas and carrot mix, diced half cooked white potatoes, and some kind of patty that was supposed to be hamburger. No seasoning was offered at any meals. This is where I was thankful that I knew how to fast and pray.

I spent the first few days of my incarceration sort of dazed, looking out the window, thinking, and reading the few books that were passed around. It wasn't long before I began to sing and make a melody in my heart to the Lord, until God lifted the burden from my heart. I noticed how many of my fellow inmates were in their teens and early twenties, most of them were under thirty. They spoke about their young children, going to court and how to "beat their cases" which involved drugs, sex trafficking, and assaults. Most of them knew each other as many of these ladies were repeat offenders. They often spoke of people they knew of on the streets because many of them came from the same circle of associates. I was amazed that a full cohort of women had a lifestyle that revolved around being in and out of jail.

I could not join in their conversations as I knew NOTHING about the streets, drugs or "the hard life." I was clueless to the jargon they spoke in their conversations.

After about a week of not knowing how long it would be before I'd be transferred to a prison, I met a young lady named Brenda who talked about how much better prison would be than this jail. I looked at her in confusion. I asked her "how is prison better than jail?" She explained she had been to prison three or four times before and it wasn't so bad. She told me how the food was better, how they had activities like soft ball, basketball, volleyball, a library and how you'd work a detail (a job) and make money around the end of your sentence. I told her, "I am not going to be here that long." I truly believed that my super attorney would be getting me out of this situation.

April 12 until my transfer May 5, 2016 - I remained in Marietta Cobb Adult Detention Center in Marietta Georgia. I had a few visitors. My older sister, Gwen; was my very first visitor. She encouraged me and told me she would be praying with me for this to be overturned. She encouraged me to trust God for his will to be done. Sherry McNair – Humphries, a good friend, and her mom Sheryl visited. Minnie Daniels, from the Nurse's ministry and Monica Denson, from the Dance ministry, at Word of Faith Family Worship Cathedral, all came as well. They all said they would leave money for me and they did.

During these three weeks, I learned that I could order snacks and personal items with money I had on my books that my visitors had brought me. On my books meant I now had a "jail" bank account. I begin to order items from the store and eat junk food. While I begin to share some of my store goods, I begin having small talk conversations with two young girls who spoke often of their cases and how worried they were. I noticed that some of the girls were crying and talking so negative. By the unction of the Holy Spirit, I was led to read my bible aloud, write out scriptures to give them and pray with them. This is where God begin to use me to teach.

It wasn't long before I started a bible study, introduced them to the word of God and formed a choir. I showed them how talking to the Lord and singing would lift the burden of their situations. Truly, I was amazed at how many had never heard the bible stories of Daniel in the lion's den, Esther, David and Goliath, and the Hebrew boys from the book of Daniel in the Bible.

I thought everybody knew these basic bible stories. My first negative experience was with a guard. I had a dramatic incident with this guard who appeared to have a personal grudge against me for no apparent reason. One of the women in the top tier cell complained to a guard that I was singing and it was disturbing her.

The guard approached me and said, with a very nasty attitude, "If you want to sing, I can put you in isolation and you can sing all you want to. Intuitively, I figured that would not be pleasant, in a soft tone I said, I would keep my singing to a minimum not to disturb anyone. She stood looking at me with the most hateful expression as if she wanted me to say more; nonverbally I remained polite as to not give her a reason to get uglier. I said nothing more and she finally left with an attitude.

The next day when we lined up to exchange out our sheets and jumpsuits, the same guard handed me the worse torn up sheets she could get her hands on and failed to give me the correct size jumpsuits. When I tried to go back up to her to ask her to exchange it, she got so ugly and yelled so loud it made me wonder how I was going to get through this. I went back to my cell and cried. This incident threw water on my spirit and dampened me severely. I laid on my mat and went to sleep. I was awakened by the Spirit of God the next day about 4:00 a.m.; I prayed so loud that everyone in the cell pod could hear. I begin to pray in the Spirit as God overtook me and everybody knew this was the Holy Ghost, by the anointing of God's presence in the place. No one said anything, not even a guard. You could hear a pin drop after God released me from praying. I didn't have any more opposition in there after that day. The remainder of my time, I read my bible, taught those who wanted to listen and taught songs to those who enjoyed singing and ushering in the presence of the Lord.

Three weeks later, about 3:00 a.m., I was awakened and told to "pack it up." Personal hygiene and my bible gifted from Prophetess Taylor was all I had.   I was then taken downstairs into a filthy, moldy holding cell, given a cold inedible breakfast and processed out to go to prison. This was a horrible experience. Here, I and six or seven others were shackled and brought out into a tight metal seat van and transported to Lee Arrendale State prison in Georgia. It was a little more than an hour ride. The entire trip was very hot and uncomfortable.

Once we were dropped inside the gated area of the prison, the van left and we were all lined up against a wall and told to go into a little building that looked like a guard shack. We were told to get behind a curtain where we had to take EVERYTHING off. We were told to face the guard, lift your breast, and spread your labia.

The prison guard shined a flash light, brighter than a gynecologist headlight in surgery and yelled, "turn around, bend over, cough, squat, cough again and spread your cheeks." I've never felt more invaded in my entire life. Even my husband had never seen those intimate parts of me.

Although, we were separated by stalls with curtains, it was still such an invasion. We had to throw away everything; bra, panties, socks, etc.. Here is where I felt I lost all identity and every shred of dignity. We were then instructed to put the original jail scrubs back on and marched over to another building where we were instructed to "fill out paperwork describing any markings, tattoos, burns, or scars." Any and all identifying marks were processed here. I'm guessing In case you were involved in another crime previously, or once you are out in the future, this was on record to identify you.

We were all corralled into the showers, six at a time and the prison guard poured de-lice shampoo on our heads and body wash into our hands. We could not handle the bottles at all. We all had to come out of the shower and sit on a bench (while our hair was soaped up) so the shampoo could work. I suppose they were making sure no one had lice or weapons hidden in their hair.

If you had on acrylic nails, or toe nail polish, you were given cotton balls with remover and made to take it off. Anything that resembled your life as a female was now stripped away. One lady had Dreadlocks she had grown for five years and had to have them all cut off.

We were then issued state underwear, socks, sports bras, t-shirts, black boots and tan looking scrubs to wear. Huge letters on the back of the t-shirt and scrubs that read, **DEPARTMENT OF CORRECTIONS**.   I was now property of the state.

After I and the entire group were clean and dressed in prison attire, we stood in line to take pictures and were issued a number. **1001747909 was who I'd become in the state of Georgia.** We were also given one combination lock.

It was my first day in state prison; I was in a world I could not understand. How did I get here? I felt I'd done nothing wrong and yet, I found myself in a cell block with hundreds of other women.   The bed space was limited so we were separated into different housing quarters. Some on C-1, C-2 and I was taken to SMU (single man units) and housed there until I was moved again into C-1.   I assume the (C) stands for cell.

Once you came into the building from the outside, the prison housing unit was a two-story brick building with a door on each end of the unit that resembled a cage from

floor to ceiling. The floors and walls were
there were no internal doors on any of the s
The only internal doors were to the broom/.
and to what was called the Day room with squa   ..ples
and plastic chairs where you could play cards or watch
TV. This door was locked until after inspection. I'll tell
you about inspections later in the story.

There was open hall space with openings to each room
as you walked down the one open corridor. Each room
had four bunk beds, eight women to a room and an
open bathroom area with three toilets stalls covered by
a curtain. It had one huge shower each person
showered alone or at least I did. On the other side of
this bathroom were four more bunkbeds, this mirrored
the entire length of the corridor. Essentially, between
each sleep room there was one huge shower, three
toilets and two stainless steel sinks which were shared
by sixteen females.

There were two small stacked lockers on top of each
other that separated each bunk bed. The locker only had
three shelves. This is all the space you had to store your
personal belongings. Although everyone had their own
combination lock for their own locker, somehow people
still managed to find a way to steal. The next wall
repeated the same line up for a total of about eight
rooms on each side of the corridor. There were 128

. living tighter than most families. Can you imagine how attitudes and hormones were flying around?

Fights consisted of a lock in a sock, Mop and broomsticks, or some females bashing the head of someone else against the cement walls. I stayed far away from the drama.

As I looked back over the last fifty-five plus years of my life, my education, trainings, certifications, places of employments, travel, churches and the running of my own business; nothing prepared me for this. In an effort to get through what was taking place, I decided to consistently keep a journal and pray every day.

The prison routine began with a head count every few hours, 06:00, 09:00, noon, and 3:00 p.m. and so on. Sometimes, they would do a random count just because they could. Everything stopped during count time. "On your feet," the guards would yell, standing at attention next to your bunk or sometimes we would line up outside our doors and "number off" nobody moved until count was correct and cleared, meaning every prisoner was accounted for, no one had broken out.

I didn't realize it then, but now that I look back over this experience, I can say, *it was good for me that I was afflicted.* Oh My God, what am I saying? Well, I hadn't taken the time as often as I should have to visit the dentist, gynecologist, optometrist or medical doctor at home, and now here; I didn't have a choice. Here, I was given an appointment slip for EVERYTHING. I had a medical appointment for a physical. It consisted of a head to toe exam, hypertension, and diabetes screening, a dental exam and cleaning, Pap smear, vision test, podiatrist, colonoscopy and we were made to exercise daily. Well, the exercise wasn't by appointment, but it was mandatory, it was titled; "yard call."

Yard call consisted of marching in boots around a field, picking dandelions or whatever you were told to do. There were some days that you could go outside and play basketball or just walk around the field at your leisure with your entire dorm. You didn't just go outdoors whenever you wanted; it was when the guards decided to let the entire cell block outside. Even in the rain or heat, sometimes we were made to go outside.

There was no heating or air conditioning anywhere in this prison's housing units but, whatever the weather, all you had was one fan per room on a tall stand or mounted on the wall in a corner. I must say that I was blessed even in this hardship. My bed was next to a wall and a window and the fan was "in my corner."

The food here was even worse than that in the county jail. It was just inedible. Once in a while there were hotdogs and pork and beans or beefy macaroni that was sometimes tolerable. The "Chow Hall" was up a hill and around the field so what little I did eat, I walked it off. I began to lose weight until I had money transferred onto my books and I could order store, meaning I could order items I wanted to eat within the limits of what was offered to purchase.

I heard someone say, we could order "packages." A food package was something your family could order, pay for, and have it sent to you but it would take four to six weeks for delivery. Packages consisted of a weight limit of items like, instant meals, snacks and beverages, food that you could enjoy.

I responded to that, by saying, "I'm not going to be here that long." So, I didn't ask my family to order anything. I believed that this was a test and I would not be in prison long. Five weeks later when packages arrived, I was mad at myself and God to be honest because I just didn't believe I would still be in the prison.

I later found out that the cell area where I was located, was called "diagnostics" and that I would be moved into something called "general population" soon. There are four women prisons in the state of Georgia. Lee Arrendale, also known as ALTO, (this is where I was incarcerated). The other three locations were called Whitworth, Pulaski and Emmanuel Women's facility.

I continued to pray: *"God, I want to go home, but nevertheless, let your will be done."* During my unstructured quiet time, women only saw me reading my bible praying and singing. They began asking me questions about the bible and asked me to pray for them. I witnessed a little bit of the drama, but I NEVER got involved with all the drama prison had to offer; lesbian relationships, stealing, fighting and smoking. I stayed far from those scenes. But I did offer prayer when led by God.

On Sundays during the early morning hours after count I began to teach others things in the bible and invited many into my room for bible study. Days later some of us made plans to have a "church service" in the day room. Of course, the devil didn't like this and begin to rear his ugly head up in opposition. A few of the women, who the devil could use, would purposely get up on Sunday to talk loudly, play cards, curse and make out when they heard me teaching the word of God. Prison church service was only allowed when outside churches came to preach in the chapel, which wasn't often.

The next week, one of the Christian women took the television cords out of both TV's so we could have church service without others interrupting by blasting the T.V. We set up the chairs like rows of pews in a church and had gathered about thirty to forty of the inmates who wanted to participate. We assembled and worshiped until the devil and his angels could only look on. The presence of God prevailed and we were able to have a wonderful time in the Lord. Spoken words, readings, singing, preaching, teaching, almost all the attendees played a role in the service. I only facilitated and encouraged each woman to use her gifts. Later, this same evening, a few "Nicodemus" type people (meaning Nicodemus from the bible that came to Jesus by night so no one would see him) came to me secretly asking for prayer. It was too funny, but actually it's not... I thank God they came seeking, even if it was behind the scene.

My best days were when I'd receive mail. Mail Call was a most important part of my evening. I always received mail, every time. People said, "Ms. Page, you need your own Post Office Box." "Wow, Ms. Page is always getting mail." This was one of the sobering factors that kept me sane. Family and friends sent letters and cards faithfully. I will forever praise God that I had not been forgotten.

I later began to relax and think what if I really have to do this three-year sentence that was pronounced on me? What if my "Super-Lawyer" can't get me out of here? I begin to order "store" and got into the routine of eating junk food. To pick up store, you had to go to an area where you walked with your platoon. You took your net bags to pick up your order. Store choices consisted of things like, personal hygiene items, chips, cookies, coffee and creamer, Kool aid, candy and sometimes you could get ice cream when it was available. You went to a window when your name was called. But you were verified by your GDC number, Georgia Department of Corrections.

One week I ordered store. I waited to be called. They had almost completed the call for pick up, and I didn't hear my name called. I went up to the window and asked "if my store was here" and was told that "I was already called and my stuff was distributed."

I was shocked and told the lady, "absolutely not, here is my empty net bag and I had not signed for anything." When she showed me the roster where my name had been signed, it was not my signature and I shut it all down. I yelled, "Hell, to the no." Somebody had pretended to be me and stole my stuff" I told an officer and everything became closed down immediately.

The officer stopped store call, closed the store window, and had everybody to line up against the fence.

He and another guard begin to search each person's net bags. Nobody was allowed to leave. As people were searched, their store slip was compared to what they had in their bags. Obviously, whoever stole it had already randomly eaten and disbursed some, gotten rid of it through others or whatever thieves do what they do. It could not be located. I didn't care how they did it. All I knew is what they were going to do was to put that $60.00 back on my books or give me my stuff. I'd almost forgotten where I was as the old Edith didn't play about her money.

The store did re-issue all that I had ordered and I left with my stuff. However, now the store was the one that had been stolen from and charges could be brought against the thieves when they were found. It's a fact somebody knew something and people talked.

Within an hour, the officers had found out, one of the inmates "working the store" had her friend to come to the window, with my number, and loaded her bag with my stuff. We all wore identification name tags on our left collar with our number printed boldly, so it was easy enough for someone to obtain my GDC number. They both went to lock down, in Isolation, for fourteen days. God knows how to avenge his own.

One Sunday night I went to chapel for a church service, I wish I could remember the name of the church that came to minister. Nevertheless, I do remember a song they sung was an old tune called, THANK YOU. I wish I could remember all the words to the song. It went something like this...

"It could have been me, outdoors, with no food and no clothes, or left alone without a friend, or just another number, with a tragic end, but you didn't see fit to let none of these things be, cause everyday by your power, you keep on keeping me and I want to say: Thank You Lord for all you've done for me."

This was the best praise and worship service I can remember. It got so good; I thought I was in church. I praised God and shouted in that chapel as if I wasn't even in prison. I truly let go and let God have his way with me that night!

I remember that it was the next day that I was told around 11:00 p.m. to, "Pack it up." That was music to my ears. I didn't know where I was going, but it was clear that I was not going into the General Population (GP) at this God-awful place. Those that were being released into the General Population at this prison were taken out during the day and because it was late at night, I knew I wasn't going into (GP) here at this prison. Once I packed up, and my belongings were accounted for, I had to hike across campus where I was processed in five weeks ago.

Still not knowing where I was going, I was walked to a long red and white looking school bus that read Department of Corrections. I was shackled at my waist, handcuffed, ankles shackled like something you see in the chain gang movies.

This was a long ride during the night. Maybe they drove us during this time because they didn't want us to see where we we're going? Or they are afraid you may tell others? Who knows? I fell asleep and woke up in Swainsboro Georgia. We arrived and waited at the gate for thirty minutes or more. Guards came out with long handled mirrors and searched under the bus. The bus guards had to get out first and lock their guns in a box BEFORE the bus entered the gate.

We were then let off the bus one at a time, unshackled and taken into another "guard shack" behind a curtained stall and stripped searched. This time, it was not as bad as the one at Alto. They didn't have flash lights nor did they make us shower and de-lice. Here was where I'd spend the rest of my despicable sentence. So, I thought.

CHAPTER 2
EMMANUEL WOMAN'S FACILITY (E.W.F.)

I arrived at Emanuel Women's Facility **June 10, 2016.** Once we were lined against the wall of the guard shack, we were introduced to the Warden, Deputy Warden and a few other staff members. We were marched in a single file line and taken into the dorm. This place was what my husband called "The Martha Stewart Camp" type prison. It didn't look like a prison. It looked more like a prep school. The fences were minimal and you could see cars driving pass. This prison was so close to the parking lot, you could throw a rock at a car and hit one. This was a minimum-security women's facility.

The fence was Emerald green, the grass was as nice as a golf course and the building was bricked, but not prison cinder-block brick. It was clean. The floors were tiled and so shiny you could see yourself like a mirror. There were six dorms with a round circular bubble where the officers sat up high watching cameras of all these circular dorms. The dorm I was taken to was called the **A** dorm.

Upon being buzzed into the Plexiglas windowed dorm entrance, the room was open with rows of about 30 bunk beds down the right and left side of the room. There was a Day room up front near the entrance with tables and chairs. There was a large colored flat screen TV mounted to the wall. As I entered into the bed area that I was assigned to, A-18, I noticed another TV mounted over the entrances into the next section of beds. There were huge ceramic 18X18 tan tiled bathrooms and showers in the back. The sinks and toilets were porcelain, not stainless steel.

After I put my things away into the locker, chow was called and everyone lined up from the front door to the back in a single file line. I didn't know anyone and the inmates that I came with on the bus from Alto, were taken to different dorms. Once I got into the chow hall, I found it to look more like a cafeteria. Clean, air conditioned, with vending machines that lined one wall and microwaves that were available. Murals were painted on the walls in the hallways and a huge floor to ceiling drawing of a tree on a wall painted with colors and letters that resembled a school for children. Some ladies smiled and no one appeared "vicious" like some of those women I'd seen in diagnostics.

I was later informed that this place is the best of all the prisons. After being here a few days, I totally understood. Staff was nicer, classes were offered, outside was a dirt track where I walked twice a day every day, unless it was raining.

There was an organized coached softball team that played against other churches, outside details, popcorn, cokes, candy bars and movies on Friday nights.

Not only did we have Store once a week with a lot of choices for food, but they also had a micro/kitchen area in the dayroom to cook, sit and eat. We had phone privileges from sunrise to sunset, scheduled Kiosk video chats with your friends and family almost any time after 4:30 p.m. We also were issued a tablet player with the ability to load songs from the Kiosk. We could send and receive emails, take photos to send out, and we had Church service once and sometimes twice a week. We had plays, arts and crafts activities, Dorm of the Week rewards, skits, a Martin Luther King Day program, Easter Communion, an active Chaplain, Kairos, Prayer Groups, GED schooling for those who needed it, online College courses, where you'd receive actual college credits. There were cap and gown graduations with commencement speakers from the outside. I'm told our State Governor once attended a GED Graduation, before my arrival. We once had a festival with a bouncy house, face painting and games for the lady's children and families who came to visit. We had all the pleasures of home, except, you were not at home.

Well, let me back up a little bit. I don't want this to sound like a pleasurable experience, but for some ladies it was. Those who were homeless, with no family, and no skills on the outside, they were "happy" to be here. Three meals a day, laundry done three times a week picked up at your door, weekly linens washed and changed, a nice library with computer usage, friendships, etc. Some people had it better here than they had it on the streets.

There was a dorm called the **H** dorm (Honor dorm). This was reserved for those who showed character of leadership, integrity and was deemed the "better" citizens of the prison. Of course, once I found this out, I wanted to know, how I could get placed into the honor dorm. I was told you have to complete an application, interview and then be recommended to move there. I also learned quickly that when you see a captain or above, you had to stop, (more like freeze) and yell out acknowledging who they were Deputy Warden G---- on deck and wait until they walked passed you and said, "carry on." It felt like I was in the military. This was a total experience that blew me away.

One day I was asleep and was awakened by a guard asking me "what's going on with you?" I had no idea what she was talking about. I was told to step out into the hallway where Deputy Warden G--- was waiting to talk to me. She asked "what's going on with you and your bunk mate?" I still had no idea what she was talking about. She told me that my bunk mate Ms. Adams had told her I was bothering her, shaking the bed unnecessarily, exercising in bed, and talking loudly. This came as a shock. I quickly learned that people will lie on you for no reason or shall I say, for their own personal gain. I was moved to **D** dorm, which I'm told was the worst of all the dorms. Upon entering the dorm, a female by the nickname of "Bear" yelled out, "She's from 60 days in (referring to the TV show). This is a TV show where someone goes into the prison to get information and then report back to the guards. I had heard of the show but never watched it. Bear said "she had seen me on this show before and started telling it to everybody, "she's 60 days in." Granted, I didn't look, act or speak like the typical inmate, so I see where they could have thought this was possible. Unlike a lot of people who go to prison, I had no history of smoking, drugs, alcohol, tattoos, cursing, revolving criminal history, and my vocabulary just wasn't prison talk. I didn't like how she was singling me out, but I just kept to myself and only spoke when I was spoken to. I kept as quiet as possible. I continued in my word, but didn't "connect" with anyone until I met Shavonne Giles. Eventually, we begin to study the bible, ate together and had nice conversations getting to know one another.

One day I called Dedric and he informed me that he had spoken to my attorney, Richard Rice, who said "I would be in prison for THREE YEARS." I felt like my heart stopped. All I could do was cry. I got into my bunk, covered my head and cried all day.

When Shavonne came in from her detail (she worked front Administration), she noticed, came over and lifted the covers. I was so distraught. I could not even talk. All I could do was cry. The worse pain I've felt since childbirth. (Another emotional time in my life that I will reserve for another book).

At the end of the day, I gathered my thoughts with the help of the Lord and Shavonne's prayers. I made a call to my sister. CYNTHIA ALWAYS TOOK MY CALLS.

Cynthia, my younger sister in Ohio, was my number one outside help. She always kept money on my books, sent cards, pictures, talked with me on the phone and I'm sure she was praying for me as well. Dedric was my strongest supporter in Georgia. Although he lives in Los Angeles, he never missed flying to Georgia to collect rent from my tenants, paid bills, taxes and payroll. He made sure everything necessary was being done as if I'd never left the business. Without Dedric and of course GOD, the business would have been swallowed alive by this catastrophe. I'm thankful for all those who sent money, cards, and pictures, messages from the ministry, packages and the like, but God, Cynthia and Dedric were and still are my main lifeline.

Eventually, I was given a detail outside weed eating and edging grass. This was something I paid someone to do back home and to find myself doing this now was life changing.

I now have so much respect for people who work out in the heat. The bugs, gasoline odors, and coming back a shade or two darker than when I left my bunk was tough. Hats off to anyone who works outdoors professionally, God bless you.

After a visit with the podiatrist for an ingrown toenail, I received a "soft shoe" profile which meant I could no longer wear those awful boots and was issued tennis shoes which also meant I could no longer work outside detail. I know, how terrible right; Laugh out loud (lol).

Eventually I was transferred to the H–Dorm and my new detail was lightweight. I was assigned to set up tables and chairs for visitation, which was only on the weekends and holidays. My job took about twenty-five minutes at the top of the morning around 6:30 a.m. and again to take down about 3:00 p.m. The rest of my time was spent reading, writing, and attending classes, church services or other activities.

To be therapeutic and help the time pass, I joined the Scrabble club, walked the track forty-five minutes to an hour almost daily, taught aerobics and worked out on the many exercise machines available to me in the gym. I taught, "Overcoming Adversities," a class based on information I received from friends, David and Sharon Beaner, from their Seeds of Love ministry. I tailored these ministry notes to meet the needs of the prisoners. I cooked, ate and slept peacefully usually every night.

God brought me to a place where I was no longer consumed with the fact that I was in prison.

This was the peace of God that surpassed all understanding. Time passed quickly it seemed, and I began to flow with the Holy Spirit on a daily basis.

It was December 31, 2016, the last day of the year and this is my conversation with GOD, and how he responded to me. I kept saying to myself. **This is the day that the Lord had made, I will rejoice and be glad in it" – Psalms 118:24.** No matter what, I made the effort to praise God through every experience. As much as I tried to keep my mind on the Lord, there were days that I reflected on how I got here, and how it just should not have happened. I was wronged, lied on, and not given a trial. Yet, I'm in prison. I now called this my Joseph experience as he was lied on by Potiphar's wife and thrown into prison. **(Genesis 39:7-20)** Yet, how could I be glad? With verifiable proof, I wasn't even on the scene when the incident occurred, but because I'm the "owner" of the business I have to go to prison? Reported to me by my employees, the incident didn't even happen as the manipulating, drug addicted client said. I thoroughly investigated the occurrence and found that my employee was not wrong in trying to help this young man, he probably saved his life; but I've found out, *even if you do everything right, you can still be wrong.* How much sense does that make?

Tragically, I have been falsely accused of (1) abuse to an elder/disabled client. He was 34 years old, not even an elder, but the "law" has it listed in this category which made it sound so bad in the news... and he was definitely not abused. (2) False imprisonment holding a person against their will (even if it is for his own good) and (3) operating an unlicensed care home. This also was not true. Documented proof that I was licensed and registered with the state of Georgia for almost 20 years, why would I need or even want to now start running an unlicensed home? Our new location wasn't even completely renovated and no one was living in this home where we were accused. I had been an outstanding, law-abiding citizen all of my life, helping so many for so long, and I sit here in prison trying to figure out, why? This was one night that I just couldn't sleep and decided to continue writing a detailed journal of everything that happened to me daily while serving this time.

CHAPTER 3

HOW IT ALL GOT STARTED IN

POWDER SPRINGS!

An inmate asked me to pray with her. After the prayer, she said, "you just do not fit in here." *What's your story? How did you get here*? I began by telling her about how I got started. I told her I owned a business called Top-of-the-Line Residential Care and Development, Inc., a company I founded in 1995. It was licensed as a personal-care home where I served mentally challenged adults in housing, therapeutic structure, and life skills training. This was my passion, this was my God-given mission dedicated to the delivery of service was my motto.

How did I even come to start this business? Well, let me back up about 25 years ago. May 18, 1995, I was working a wonderful job as a Registered Nurse in Hospice through the Grady Health System in Atlanta Georgia. I was walking to the office from the car and I heard the Lord speak to me and say *"quit your job."* It was such a clear and audible sound I looked around me, didn't see anyone and kept walking. The closer I got to my job I heard the voice again, very clearly say *"quit your job."*

I loved my job and the families I served; there was no reason to quit. I was making great money, day shift hours, loved the patients and was genuinely happy with the service I provided to families. I built great relationships with families that I still have to this day.

I had no reason to quit.   Nevertheless, I knew it was God. It was so clear, when I got up the stairs to my office, I immediately grabbed a box, placed all my things on my desk in the box and handed my badge to my supervisor on the way out. I left; no explanation, no two-week notice, I just quit. I left just like that. I know this sounds wrong. However, it was important to me to obey God. This was over 20 years ago and I still value obeying God's voice because **1st Corinthians 2:5 says: That your faith should not stand in the wisdom of men, but in the power of God.**

On the drive home, I begin to cry and say, Lord, why? Why would you have me to quit my job, what am I going to do? What will I do? How will I ever get another job? How will I get a reference based on how I just quit my job? Only God knew I would never need another job. Little did I know God was now my new employer.

As I continued driving toward my house, my tears were so thick and heavy; I could barely see to drive. How will I pay my bills?   Then I heard the Lord say *"give up this house and give away everything in it."* Again, because I know the voice of God and have a relationship and history with being obedient, I let go of the house, and everything in it.

I called my oldest nephew and offered him for free, my beautiful bedroom set I had purchased at an estate sale in Alpharetta. It was a state-of-the-art cream colored, lacquer finish indescribably beautiful, seven-piece bedroom set. It had twinned mirrored armoires and mirrored head boards with a radio and cassette deck for music inside.   I got this from a couple that had purchased it from Italy. I was also to give away my stainless-steel kitchen appliances and all the other breath-taking pieces I'd acquired to fill my double-faced fireplace home. I was leasing a home in Creek Wood Hills where I felt like I was living the life.   I knew of a bible story about a rich young ruler and did not dare walk in his footsteps by not obeying when Jesus told him to sell all that he had to follow him.

I said to God, now where am I going to live? He replied; *go live with your mother.* I responded out loud, "in the projects?" God, you want me to park my $30,000 car in the meadows, a place where it's so bad that the police don't even want to go? There was a police precinct in the middle of Lakewood Meadows but again, I obeyed. I gave away EVERYTHING in my house, packed my car only with personal belongings and drove to my mom's apartment in Lakewood Meadows. I walked in and said, "Hey mom, I'm moving in." She didn't ask me any questions. I just went into her second bedroom, put my few things away and went to work out at the Run-N-Shoot on Stewart Avenue, now Metropolitan Parkway. It wasn't two weeks later that God set me up in business, where I've been employed by him for the last twenty years. Well, let me explain further.

My son Travis, who's now deceased one year ago today; July 27, 2018, was very much an anointed musician. He played the organ and keyboard like no other. I'm not saying that because I was his mother, anyone who heard him can attest to this statement. He could play every key on the board and made that music sound heavenly. It was a Friday night and a minister at a church in Atlanta was coming to pick him up to play. I told Travis, "I think I'll go with you." As we drove to church, the minister was telling us about a home he had in Smyrna and how he was about to have it turned into a personal care home with a lady by the name of Annette Carter in Powder Springs, who had multiple homes. For some reason I said, "Why are you giving the home to her if she already has so many? Give it to me, I'd like to do a Personal Care home." I had never heard of Powder Springs and I knew nothing about running a business. It just sounded like a good idea. Now, I know it was the leading of the Lord.

I didn't know anything about the Personal Care Home business and never had a desire to "run a care home" but I just said it.   Minister Maddox responded, "Well, you can meet her and ya'll can take it from there". After the service was over this same night, we drove to the home of Ms. Annette Carter in Powder Springs and we begin to talk as if we'd known each other for years. Now, over twenty years later, we're still friends to this day. It was getting late and Annette said, "You know what, there's a home here in Power Springs that's closing tonight and I know the owner. She may let you have this house after these other people move out." You guessed it; we drove about five minutes to the home at 4321 Atlanta Street, Powder Springs Georgia. This is where history was made.

As I walked up the ramp, the people were rolling patients out in wheel chairs. When I walked into the house, I understood why it was being closed. It was a hot mess. It was filthy, stinky, and infested with roaches. I would not put a dog in this home. It was so disgusting. I thought to myself, how could a home ever get in this shape?

As the people were packing up and moving people out, Ms. Karolyi, the owner of the home walked in, obtained the keys from the previous tenants and walked around looking. Annette Carter introduced me to her. Again, I knew nothing about business, but once we started talking and I begin talking like I would take over the home, clean it up and make a nice business of it, Ms. Karolyi responded to me. "Well if you want it, it's yours" as she put the keys in my hand. No lease, no contract, no money, no questions asked, just gave me the keys.

This was my introduction and the beginning of the start of God's business called, <u>Top of the Line Residential Care and Development, Inc.</u> which I ran for **twenty years**.

I went home to my mom's apartment. I told her what had transpired that night and she was so excited, she said "let's go see it right now." I said "mom, it's late, it's after midnight and that place is filthy." Mom said "let's go clean it up." She got a broom, mop, a bucket, bleach, 409, Mr. clean, trash bags, and pine-sol and headed to the car. Mom had plenty of cleaning supplies, and was a master at cleaning. I was anxious about it as well, so we got into the car and went over to the home.

We walked in, looked around and mom and I begin to anoint every room over the door-post with oil. We walked through and prayed, and then begin to pull up carpet, rolled it up and dragged it outside. We scrubbed the floors, walls, doors, bathrooms, threw away every sheet, towel, curtains, dishes and mattresses. I mean we tossed everything except the bed frames and two chairs for us to sit. We bleached down everything good including the cabinets and toilets from the ceiling to the floor. It was now just about day break and we were exhausted. We fell asleep sitting up in the chairs. We slept until the phone rang and woke us up.

The phone call was from Kennestone Hospital asking if we had any empty beds available for a patient. I explained that "the home you are calling has closed; however, my name is Edith Page. I am a registered nurse and I will be opening the home very soon. I would love to come and assess the patient." We finished up quickly and drove to Kennestone` Hospital and met what would become our very first patient. I love this guy to this day. I remember his very words. Edie are you taking me home with you?" "Yes Tony, I replied, you are going home with me today."

After the interview, the social worker asked me how much do we charge? As I said I knew nothing about business, I did not know what to charge. I heard the Holy Ghost say in my spirit $800. So, I said, "eight hundred dollars" and she replied, "great, you can take him with you today he has $830." Mom and I left the hospital with this patient and $800. We stopped at Home Depot and bought paint, brushes, mini blinds for the window and peel and stick tile for the floor. We went to

Walmart and bought sheets, towels and other supplies. We spotted a small mattress shop in a plaza and made a deal to buy all our mattresses from him, if he'd work with us on delivery and give us credit and time to get the house completed. He did it. The man delivered one mattress that very day and the rest as we completed each room.

By the time we'd completed everything necessary to serve this patient, the phone ranged again. This time, it was Annette calling with a patient for me. Her name was Jan. She also was paying $800 dollars.

Mom and I continued to get another room ready. With Jan's $800 dollars, the next day we continue fixing up the house. We purchased dishes, pots and pans, supplies we needed and food. This pattern continued every day until the house was full. God gave me a business before I even knew I needed a license. Two weeks after quitting my job, May 18, 1995, I was now in business for God. May 31 was the day I began this quest officially and made an application for a Personal Care Home license.

I received a call from Andre Westfield with the Georgia Department of PERSONAL CARE HOMES wanting to come and inspect the house. I packed up all of our clients in a van I recently purchased and took all of them with my mom to Golden Corral to eat. While they were eating, I came back to the house to meet Andre.

He walked through this home and gave me a score of 99 on the house. When I asked why I didn't get 100, he said your water temperature was not the correct temperature. I didn't know anything about water heaters. I looked at it and turned a red knob upward and continued talking to him. Just before he was getting ready to leave, I asked him to check the water temperature again. He did and it was a perfect 120°.

He scratched out the 99 and gave me 100. I was licensed almost overnight.

Mom and I took turns doing everything that needed to be done. By this time, we were literally living in the Personal Care home 24 hours a day. We shared a room together and my son, Travis had a room as well. We only went to the apartment to check on it periodically until a cousin of mine needed somewhere to live. My cousin stayed at the apartment and maintained it until she no longer needed it.

For about two years, mom and I ran this home together with no other staff. Mom cooked, cleaned, washed clothes, and I handled the medications, managed doctor's appointments and the personal care of the clients. We went to Bible studies, church services, we took them bowling, shopping and out to the movies on a regular basis. These twelve clients and we were one big happy family, in my 15 passenger van.

Every time the state would come out to inspect, we received nothing but the highest compliments. How nice and clean it was, how good our food smelled cooking. Mom did not (and still don't) believe in canned food, she said "her beans, corn, and peas, had to be fresh." She would soak beans at night and let them cook half the day. Mom kept the house immaculate and always had good food on the table.

She gave them choices as to what they wanted to eat. She never went by the menu I prepared. Mom always felt like this is their home and they should have whatever they wanted. Mom might cook oatmeal, cream of wheat, and grits for breakfast because we were top-of-the-line and she wanted everybody to be happy. Every Sunday pancakes, bacon and eggs, sausage, milk, juice and coffee were served; after this we usually all went to church.

The client's and their families were happy to have their loved ones with us. They told us how happy their loved ones were living there, and most said, "This is the nicest care home my loved one has ever lived in." Mentally challenged clients often went from home to home when they did not live in the institutions. (Now unfortunately, the jails are serving as the new institutions). Here I was, 35 years old running my own business. As we began to make money, I began to hire staff so mom and I could get a break.

My first hire was Delva; a lady from England had two children in college and sent all of the money she earned to them. She lived in and had her own room but left to be with her friends who picked her up on the weekends. Then I hired a weekend staff person and mom and I moved out. I was naive and didn't realize everybody didn't work as hard as mom and I did. I made some mistakes, but learned from them all.

Over a period of ten to fifteen years, I had hired and fired about 40 different people over my years in business. (I still have their files). Most people want a job, but they don't want to work.

I was looking for others to do as I did; until I realized that this was my baby, my passion, my ministry and no one can do it like God gave me to do. I still have 95 percent of our reviews from the state showing that we were indeed TOP OF THE LINE, very much superior to other care homes our size. No disciplinary reports, no infractions, no fines, no plan of corrections had to be done as long as I and mom were running things. It was only when I hired managers, administrators and staff who did not follow all policies and procedures that we even began to have some difficulties. But still nothing major. We were NEVER EVER accused of any type of abuse or neglect to our clients.

As we obeyed God, clients begin to get "better." Our reputation grew to the point where we had clients coming from as far as California.

If Top of the Line couldn't do it, it couldn't be done. This was said by an Attorney Ms. McManus, a person who often made referrals to our home from the courts.

Clients no one else could handle, difficult clients that no one else wanted to deal with, became our "brand." We took on the clients who needed special attention, one on one care, and over time they would be **healed** to the point where they didn't even need much personal care anymore. They no longer qualified to be in a personal care home, as they became self-sufficient, as we taught them the therapeutic life skills needed and medication management to be independent.

I asked God "where do we go from here?" The clients have no rental history, no credit history, no employment history, and they have no family that can or will take them in. No family who had the time or energy to deal with some of their idiosyncrasies that they still had. When you deal with mental illness; still at the root, you will see "fixed delusions" that they will always believe. Many were able to live semi - independent, in spite of their delusional thinking. Some actually believed that they are/were Jesus Christ or Elvis Presley. Some of them thought people in the TV were talking to them. They could cook, clean, wash, shop, take their own medications, make their own appointments and handle all the life skills they were taught and some held down gainful employment. My mission had been accomplished, to teach them the life skills needed to live productive lives in the community and they no longer qualified to live in personal care. They only needed "supportive" living arrangements.

One morning I had a dream. I woke up in a weird, strange, transcendental state, almost like I was hypnotized, something I'd never experienced and I didn't understand what it meant.

What I saw in the dream were dilapidated boarded-up buildings. Days later, as I was pulling out of the driveway one morning, I went into what I call a transcendental state of mind. As I pulled into the street, I was directed to drive my car in the direction that I was hearing in my spirit. (These are the directions as God showed me). Turn left out of the driveway, a right at the first stop sign, one block up another right, then an immediate left. One block up, then turn left again. Then, at the next stop sign, turn right, and at the second driveway turn left. I came to a stop and I came out of the trance.

When I came out of this "trance," I saw the dilapidated boarded-up buildings that I had seen in my dream. I got out of my car and saw a man on the roof of a brick duplex nailing and there was a sign in the yard that said for sale.

I told the man I'm buying this building as is, you can come down now. After I said it, I now realize (years later) how crazy I must have sounded.

I'm sure this was God talking through me. I had never purchased an apartment building in my life. The man looked at me like I was crazy and continued nailing. I pulled the sign up out of the yard, threw it into the back of his pick-up truck and I repeated, "I said you can come down now, I'm buying this building as is."

The man came down wiping his hands on a navy-blue dotted handkerchief, looking at me very strangely. I asked him what he wanted for the building and I think he said something like "$75,000 or $80,000." I said, "I'll give you $60,000 for it." He walked away from me continuing to wipe his hands. I pulled out my cell phone and I called the number on the For-Sale sign. It was Buckhead brokers. When the lady answered the phone, I told her the address where I was and what I wanted to do.

She asked me "how much are you offering and I told her $60,000." She replied, "Oh no, don't waste your time, he just turned down $65,000 last week". I replied to her, "I'm on my way to your office now." "I want to put this under contract. I'm on my way" and I hung up the phone. When I arrived at her office, we completed the contract, faxed it over to the seller and we continued to talk. Before the ink was dried good on the paper, the man had signed it, accepting my offer and faxed it back.

That's not even the amazing part. I showed up to the closing with postdated personal checks. No cashier checks, no cash, just my own personal postdated checks as my down payment. He must have owned the building outright because he accepted those postdated checks and owner financed for me until I was able to pay it off in a very short time.

The next building, I purchased, was directly across from this one. It was boarded up with abandoned cars parked around the side of it. I called the realtor's name on the sign and spoke to Joan. One of the nicest ladies I've ever met.

When she came out to meet me at the property, she told me it was a "HUD" property and that I needed to already have finance lined up because it's not sold like a typical home. The sale would be based on "bids" and you only have a few days to produce the money. She asked me what my bid was on this property; I gave her the numbers that I heard God speak to me. Somewhere in the neighborhood of $43,654.19. It just didn't make a lot of sense, but I told her to write it just like I said it, please.

When we arrived at the Federal Richard D. Russell building, in downtown Atlanta, for the opening of the bids; my bid won by a few dollars and some change. I knew that was God, this was amazing and I begin to praise God right there in the federal building on the elevator. I was shouting and praising God. This would be the second duplex God gave me to fix up and prepare to receive clients who no longer needed to receive personal-care.

Now being that it was a HUD property, you have to pay for it within 72 hours. I needed a cashier check for the exact amount and I didn't have any of it. I said, "Ok, Lord where am I getting this money from? He led me to call one of my client's family members. I asked him "if I could borrow about $45,000? I told him I'm on my way to your house now to pick it up." When I arrived at the home of William Clifford Voyles, I told him what I had done and that I needed the money today. With a puzzled facial expression, he said, "today?" He looked at me a little strange and said, "I would not do this for my twin brother and I don't know why I'm doing this for you today." He pulled out his check book and wrote me a check for that amount. I went to the bank, got a cashier check, took it to the realtor and that's how I got that second building.

The clients were "healing" fast and I needed additional housing for them. I didn't think I was ready to purchase another property and didn't have the money to fix it up. Therefore, I went to rent a duplex, another property behind the one I already owned. The lady took my application but came back and told me, I'm sorry; your credit did not pass approval. I cannot rent to you." I said okay, I guess that means I'll just have to buy it.

I told the lady who I was and what I wanted to do. I said, "I can pay you $5,000 a month for 12 months and that's a total of $60,000. This is what I'm going to pay for this two-bedroom, 1 bath duplex. No realtor, no fees, no closing cost, just you and me from seller to buyer."

I put my foot on the bumper of her jeep and on my knee; I wrote out twelve, $5,000.00 checks, gave them to her and instructed her to "deposit the checks on the 5th of each month as they are dated."

I said, to her, "you keep the keys, keep your tenants, keep the rent and I'll see you in 12 months to collect the deed" and I left the property. A few days later, she called me and said, "Honey, if you really want this property this bad, I'm going to let you have it. Meet me at my attorney's office" and the rest is history. I don't know how or why she did it with my bad credit; but she worked it out and I still own all these properties to this day and almost a dozen others still serving those in need.

God worked wonders day after day, month after month, year after year. To date, God has blessed me to be voted Business Women of the Year by the Cobb County Democratic NAACP under the presidency of Deanna Bonner. Wells Fargo Bank awarded me with one of the Community Leadership Awards for Community Service in the amount of $1.000.00 at an annual breakfast four years in a row. My company was awarded $10,000 from Georgia Power, a Southern Power company two years consecutively. I was also gifted a complete 100 percent scholarship by Kennesaw State University Continuing Education Department where I have earned my Certification in Gerontology.

Over 15 years in business, making a difference in the lives of hundreds of clients, no disciplinary reports, no discrepancy's, no infractions, no fines, not even an accusation serving the community. At most, there were a few plan of corrections that I "corrected" and continued to run an efficient, Top of the line business, I had been dedicated to the delivery of service. *Until*...

I received a call asking me to take on a very difficult client. This client needed individualized attention which he was given until he decided he no longer wanted the therapeutic structured environment we offered. I was accused in 2013. but the case was thrown out of court by Judge Bodiferd before he retired. It was tossed out again in 2014 and again in 2015.

I didn't understand how this case could keep surfacing after it was reportedly "thrown out" as I had thought. One lawyer explained it to me like this. "If they say you were wearing red and didn't get anywhere, now they can come back and say you were wearing blue and start the case over." This made no sense to me. Nevertheless, after going back and forth three years, there was finally, an unexpected indictment March 2016. Then, before I knew what happened, I'm off the map and in prison, April 12, 2016.

In my heart, I believe there was a "political agenda" to this entire situation; I believe it was calculated to Scandalizing my name, to prevent me from running for office. I'd already run for State Representative House District 36 in Cobb county in the past and came very very close to winning against an incumbent who'd been in office for several years. A few years ago, I had also "announced" that I would be running for mayor. I truly believed somebody just didn't want me and Hillary Clinton teaming up. Lol.

During the time imprisoned, I have never felt "bound." I may have had to wear handcuffs and shackled at the ankles during transport, but never was I spiritually bound. Thank you, Jesus! Our conversation and story ended. She looked at me and said, "I knew I was right about you!" You really don't belong here. After telling her the story, I begin to re-live the pain of it all over again.

I began recalling on scripture to help me get through my feelings of this strange and seemingly dark place in my life. **Roman 15: 4** was the first scripture my eyes fell on in the bible in the New Year. At that moment while lying in my bunk, God already had a plan, a plan that didn't involve requesting my permission to do so**. "For whatever things where written afore time, were written for our learning, that we through the patience and comfort of the scriptures might have hope."** Lord I need hope right now. Here I was seemingly alone in this world at a place I had no knowledge of and never thought I'd experience. My prayers to God continued unceasingly.

For this New Year, I had to rest assured that God was telling me to patiently continue to study his word, continue to be comforted and keep the hope of what his word says. But Lord, I just received a ten-year sentence, three to serve in prison, and have been accused of something I am not guilty of. I was trying to walk by faith but there were days I was just feeling some kind of way I cannot even describe.

The word of God gave me the confidence to face the days, the weeks, the months and years to come and I vowed to continue to read the bible daily. But Lord, help me understand. Before reading the bible this morning, I had to think back to the beginning of this situation. What happened?

It was Mr. Arthritic Pain, a 34-year-old adult, housed in my program Top of the Line Residential Care and Development, Inc. I was in the process of opening another personal care home going through the transition of renovation. A very nice almost $300,000 home, just a few streets away from the current licensed personal care home; housing for more clients. This was a new facility that had not yet opened. There were no residents living there at this location as it was under major renovation. Scaffolding, five-gallon paint buckets, sheet rock, plywood, and building supplies everywhere throughout the house. It was evident during the investigation that no one lived there, but they still charged me with operating an unlicensed home because the client actually was at that house (for other reasons), the day the incident occurred. He did NOT live at this house. Even worse, because he was taken back to the house where he lived, (we were also charged with kidnapping).

At the home where he lived, (my office was also in this location); I was typing the report to take with him to the hospital, he begged and begged me not to send him to the hospital. His exact words were, "Edith you know what they do to people like me in the mental hospital". "Please don't send me there". This was a very intelligent young man with a substance abuse history and very manipulative. I feel now that I made an error in Judgement, but according to the plans of God, things went as they were supposed to. I hope there is a question and answer period at the pearly gates. Lol...

I served difficult disturbed mentally ill residents in the past, I've seen how God used me in the past to get people delivered before; I felt it was an opportunity for GOD to show himself strong to "deliver" this seriously challenged young man. Even before taking him as a client, I and my husband went to the home of his parents, (who sought me out); we obtained his history, and completed an assessment based on what they told us.

In addition to listening to my staff and two trips to Albany Georgia to meet this client, talk with him and his current caregiver, I knew he'd be a challenge. I was and still am counting on the God that I serve to deliver him.

The God that answers by fire, the God that has never lost a case, I'm still counting on him to avenge me of my adversary.

While some said, I shouldn't have taken on this troublesome client, "I'm not afraid to jump into the deep end because my life guard walks on water." (I saw that on a sign somewhere). Jesus still saves, and the blood still works, regardless of what it looks like! Anyway, I still believe when this is all over, God will be glorified and this young man will be totally delivered. I'll definitely write about it in my next book.

I still have the audio and video recordings that the Judge deemed "inadmissible" even though it could prove so much, God knows and I'm sure the day will come when he will show himself strong and I will be vindicated.

This is a little side bar off topic of being imprisoned, but it does speak to how I thought my life was going to go... before I go into the next chapter of **Life's detours**. *Let me share with you how I had planned my life to go, here is a speech I wrote when I was about 19 yrs. old attending college. I was a contestant in the Miss Black elegance pageant and again in the Miss Black Ohio pageant. I wish I could say I won, but I did place in the top 10 out of 50 of us young ladies. Now, use your imagination, I walked the run way as I was speaking and timed it just right to end the speech as I came to the end of the 30 foot runway stage. This was written over 40 yrs. ago.*

The speech was titled; **I'M GOING TO HAVE IT ALL**.
It went like this:

GOOD EVENING, I AM EDITH PAGE; FOR THOSE OF YOU WHO DON'T KNOW ME,

YOU WILL BY THE TIME I LEAVE THIS STAGE.

I'M A STUDENT AT THE UNIVERSITY OF TOLEDO AND MEDICAL COLLEGE OF OHIO

I WILL SOON HAVE MY BACCHELORETTE DEGREE IN NURSING,

I'M GOING ALL THE WAY WITH EDUCATION, I'M GETTING MY MASTERS AND MY Ph.D.

I'M GONNA HAVE IT ALL.

MY HOME WILL BE BUILT FROM THE GROUND, 4 BEDROOMS AND TWO FULL BATHS

A FOUR CAR GARAGE AND A BUILT IN SWIMMING POOL, AND MY CLOTHES, THE BEST OF SILKS AND CASHMERES.

I'M GONNA HAVE IT ALL

PRESTIGE IS ALSO IMPORTANT TO MY PROFESSIONAL GROWTH AND DEVELOPMENT, THAT'S WHY I'M 3RD VICE PRESIDENT FOR THE TOLEDO COUNCIL OF BLACK NURSES INC, AND CHAIR PERSON FOR THE LABOR & INDUSTRY COMMITTEE FOR THE TOLEDO NAACP AND ALSO A MEMBER OF THE PRESTIGIOUS NAACP INVESTIGATION COMMITTEE;

*I AM TRUTH PERSONIFIED, DIGNITY GLORIFIED, AND I'M GOOD, I AM MATTER IN MOTION WITH SOUL AND DEPTH , A POSTIVE PERSON WITH A VISION THAT WILL PROVIDE INSIGHT FOR MY PEOPLE, YES, **I'M GONNA HAVE IT ALL.***

THE DEGREES, THE PRESTIGE, THE FINE HOME AND CLOTHES LIVIN THAT GOOD LIFE, YEA...

I'M GONNA HAVE IT ALL*... OR WILL I? .... PAUSE;*

WHAT ABOUT MY SOUL?

WHAT DO I REALLY HAVE IF I'M NOT LIVING MY LIFE FOR CHRIST? NOTHING! I HAVE NOTHING WITHOUT CHRIST, BECAUSE I KNOW, CHRIST STRENGHTENS ME AND IS GIVING ME THE WILL AND THE POWER TO ACHIEVE HIS PURPOSE ;

I REALIZE THERE'S NO SUCCESS WITHOUT SACRIFICE AND THERE IS NO GAIN WITHOUT PAIN , AND EVERYTHING THAT IS NICE, HAS IT'S PRICE, BUT WITH THE HELP OF JESUS CHRIST, AS SURE AS CHRIST ROSE FROM THE DEAD ONE EARLY MORNING, I'M SURE; I TOO, WILL RISE ABOVE,

BECAUSE I HAVE GOT WHAT IT TAKES, MY LORD AND SAVIOR JESUS CHRIST THANK YOU!

I MADE AN ABOUT FACE TURN AND SWITCHED OFF THE STAGE AS I RECEIVED A STANDING OVATION...

NOW, BACK TO TODAY.

LIFE'S DETOURS CONTINUES.... CHAPTER 4

CHAPTER 4
LIFE'S DETOURS!

My first thought was to tell MY STORY, the details, the facts, the lies, of how this entire situation came about. As I begin to write this book, I started with "here's exactly what happened." However, the Lord spoke. Of course, GOD gave me the wisdom and insight as to share what HE WANTS the audience to read. My Story for his Glory. Therefore, I'll start where God begins to transition my thinking greater that I could even imagine.

It was New Year's Eve! A few of the female inmates glued glitter to their butts with the words happy new year and streaked up and down the halls naked. The guards didn't do a whole lot of watching us on H-Hall since we were "Honorable women," right?

A few of us Christians gathered into a class room for Watch Night service and prayed. This was another powerful growth point for me. God spoke to me with directions and instructions for the new life I was about to embark upon. As I journaled daily allow me to share with you so many of my thoughts and experiences, while inside prison.

From the writings of my Journal......

January 1, 2017 - The first day of the year, another opportunity to get it right. **"This is the day the Lord has made, I will rejoice and be glad in it."** Romans 15:4 assures me that **for whatsoever things were written aforetime were written for our learning, that through patience and comfort of the scriptures, I might have hope.**

I begin to think, for this to be the very first scripture my eyes fell on when I opened my bible today, I'm resting assure that God is telling me to patiently continue to study his word, continue to be comforted in the scriptures and keep hope of what his word says. You might be asking yourself, why I rely so much on the bible scriptures. It's a book written by man, right? Not to me. I've tested and tried it. It's proven itself to me, time and time again throughout my lifetime.

Why am I so into the word of God? *I Kings 8:56: says there hath not failed ONE WORD of all His good promise, ...* The word of God gives me <u>confidence</u> of what ALL my days, my weeks, my months, and years to come will ALWAYS be like. This daily walk makes me SURE OF MY STEPS as long as I am following his lead.

Matthew 5:18 ...till heaven and earth pass away, not one jot or one tittle shall in no wise pass away from the Law till ALL BE FULLFILLED.

January 2, 2017, 7:15 a.m. - Another day that the Lord has made, I will rejoice and be glad in it no matter the weather, (it is raining); no matter the attitudes; (they are negative all around me). [Just one of many examples: there is "a heavy discussion" over the use of the bathroom this morning.] No matter my work detail, (someone sent for me early to come set up for visitation at 5:30 a.m. and my detail doesn't start for another hour), well... Hallelujah anyhow! I have to survive within these walls, so I went to do my detail early and set up.

I was one of the lucky ones. My entire detail took about 90 minutes/day for the entire weekend/holiday combined while other inmates worked the kitchen, maintenance, outside details, and other duties 8 hours a day, five days a week. Therefore, I will not complain. I thank you God things are as well as they are. Glory to God, I will not allow the devil to steal the little joy I still have today. Sometimes what seems to look bad isn't as it appears.

I didn't have the opportunity to talk to my family on the outside before coming here except for my baby sister, Cynthia. What a gem she was. Cynthia made sure I always had money on my books, encouraged me with beautiful cards and kept up with what I was doing.

January 3, 2017 - 8:30 a.m. - I woke up late. It was 5:30 a.m. I showered, groomed, dressed and brushed my teeth. There in the mirror, I saw it again, **1001747909**. That was me. I really didn't have a name in here. Everything that occurred or happened to me was documented in the record under that number.

I tried to keep my head clear no matter what was going on around me. I was allowed to have a tablet, with the capacity to play music, e-mail and send pictures, this helped me a great deal.

Time moves on regardless as to where you are or the circumstance. I emailed my mom a birthday card and letter. Today is all about the will of the father.

As I listened to the music, I made my bed, cleaned out my locker and even read my scripture. As I read my Bible, in **Daniel Chapters 1 – 3**, it reminds me of God's power and how I must keep my faith in him.

It is Gods job to give me the revelation of what he wants me to speak and when I am called upon to answer a question, a request, or to preach a sermon. What I hear Him saying to me today is; His promise to keep all malice and guile away from me. That is my prayer today. It's almost time for inspection and I am ready. Inspection consist of having all three shelves of clothing neatly folded a certain way, while you stand at attention.

I hope and pray today that this will be the last day of Reentry class. This is a class of twelve weeks designed to help an inmate re-enter society, learn interview skills, and resume writing which was stuff I already knew. With my being an employer, I already knew this information. Therefore, I helped with this class by adding questions like; why should I hire you and not the other applicant who has the same credentials?

Tell me about your work experiences and this time gap of unemployment? Tell me about your weaknesses and strengths? I had been in the class for several weeks now and was helping to "teach it" at the same time. We did "mock" interviews, resume writing and we made collages to be used once we were released.

I had been told by my case coordinator, once my case plan is closed, I'm positioned to be out of here. Nevertheless, whatever the Father says its yea and Amen. I am trying not to think about the one-third of the "time" that the inmates tell me that you serve before you are released. However; it's hard not to think about it. That it is all the women here talk about is their TPM (Tentative Parole Month) and their PED, (Parole Eligibility Date). The most discussed question in the entire prison was, you got a date yet?

I'm excited about my birthday this coming Saturday, January 7th. I have to keep my mind clear to enjoy it. I will be 57 years young as my mom would say. Tomorrow my mom will turn 83 years young and it only seems like yesterday. The one thing I will always remember about my mom is that she always has a song in her mouth and blesses the name of the Lord at all times. She taught me to love God first with all my heart, mind, soul and strength. She also taught me to treat others the way I want to be treated. Momma, I thank God for this day, another birthday for you and me.

I pray there are many, many more birthdays. These walls may be between us but God has a plan for me to travel with the gospel and you're going to travel with me momma. "My situation is not my destination only preparation for what God has for me." I heard this saying from a counselor.

I attended Choir rehearsal today. It was alive with the presence of God again. Ms. Shavonne Giles is now the choir director and she believes in letting God rule, reign, and have his way. Singing in the choir is helping me feel some sense of normalcy. But what's normal about living within these walls, Lord? What did I do to deserve serving time for doing nothing wrong? Trying to help someone who hurt me? Feeding him and he bit my hand. I tried not to think of my sentence. I try to face one day at a time. Nevertheless... this is not an easy pill to swallow.

While I am in here, I'm trying not to think about what's going on outside because there's nothing I can do about it anyway. I've always been the go-to person, so who is everybody going to now? Maybe, this is God's way of showing me, I'm not invincible – that is God's job. People, friends, family, clients always needed to call on me. Now, they all need to learn to call upon the Lord for themselves!

January 4, 2017 – 5:30 a.m. Good Morning Jesus. Happy Birthday mom! These are the thoughts running through my mind:

"Good morning Jesus. So glad you're here.

You bring joy bells when you are near

Lift all my burdens, lift all my fears

Good Morning Jesus, so glad you're here."

Just yesterday my friend and choir director, Shavonne Giles, just moved back into this Honor dorm. An Honor dorm is a place where inmates were housed for "good character." Wow, I'm so glad. She's real in her belief. We can now sing, pray and study the word of God together again. Last night, she joined us on the Jericho walk. I thank God for people who are real.

"This is the day that the Lord has made. I will continue to rejoice and be glad in it!" Nothing shall separate me from the love of God.

I feel so uncertain this morning, but I don't know why? I went to sleep at a decent hour, about 9:30 p.m. As always, I lay down with the Lord on my mind. I'm going to write letters now and get them in the mail this morning when I go to breakfast. The mailbox is in the chow hall.

10:00 a.m. – I didn't get all the letters done. I'm going to finish them tonight. I made Cynthia, my sister, a Birthday card; and wrote a very immediate and urgent request to the Warden to allow my mom to visit on Saturday. Prayer was great tonight as well. At the Jericho Walk, Kairo was cancelled for some unknown reason. Kairo is an inside prison ministry of women from all over the states. They only minister to incarcerated people. Kairo is a three-day spiritual journey, Friday, Saturday and Sunday from 7:30 a.m. in the morning until about 3:00 p.m.

Again, I am not sure what was going on outside these walls. I know my husband was sentenced to six months and he went into custody the same day I did, but not with me. His daughter, Lesette, took him to jail. He turned himself in the same day my Godson, Dedric was in court with me. While I was in jail waiting to be taken to the pod (cell), I saw my husband dressed in navy scrubs sitting in a wheel chair on the side of the jail holding area designated for the males. I sat on the side with women in orange and he sat there on the other side in blue. We never said a word to each other. I was angry, mad, extremely upset with him for reasons I'm not even quite sure about? My husband with no criminal history at all, sentenced because we are married and he was considered my "business partner." Although I wake up every day with the Lord on my mind, somehow my mind keeps rolling back to how and why this all happened.

January 5, 2017 - 10:37 a.m. - Another day that the Lord has made. Another opportunity to get it right. "In him I move, I live and have my being." Lord, my prayer is that I continue in your word. With all that is taking place in front of me and behind closed doors, daily will I seek thee. One of my favorite sayings is, in him, not me, no longer I, but thee. **Philippians 2:13 - For it is God which worketh in me both to will and to do of his good pleasure.**

Father, this is my prayer for the day!

"Father, I thank you for this day. I will rejoice and be glad in it. My soul doeth make her boast in the lord. The humble shall hear thereof and be glad. Oh, magnify the lord with me. Let us exalt his name together. For the

Lord is good, his mercy is everlasting and his truth endureth to all generations. I love God; I love the word of God so much that it pours out of me. Anytime I have a question, I want the answer to be based on the word of God. Not what I think or what I feel or what anybody has to say about it.

"God, daily will I cry out to thee. I don't ever want one day to go by that I have not consulted you about it. Lord, you are in total control. I will not do anything without your consent. In fact, my desire is your desire. I want what you want, nothing more and nothing less. I give my whole life to you. Lord, I do feel weak and weary, but I know you are here with me. Guiding me and giving me strength to face another day. But Lord, I am still trying to understand what it is you want me to learn from all of this?"

My mind reflects back on my husband, my child, my church, its members and the outside world. These are the memories that keep me going. I have turned over my entire life to you, Lord.

I continue to pray:

Lord, I will trust and obey you 100%. Father, I'm yours, everything I've got, everything I am, and everything I'm not. I'm yours Lord, try me and see.... See if I can be completely yours! In you I live, in you I move, in you I have my being I will not start to move unless I move in you. 100% of the time I will serve you. This is my heart desire! Amen.

God you wrote the end from the beginning. So, it's already done. Lord, my prayer is that I continue in your word daily.

January 6, 2017 – It's been a great day! I was however disappointed with visitation. But, it's a great day. I was tearful that mom was not approved to visit me because she has no birth certificate. In 1934, (children who were born at home, names were written in the bible, she has no birth certificate). I really had looked forward to that visit. But it's a great day anyway. I got on the scale and realized I have gained back all the weight I had lost. Yet, still another disappointment, but, it's a great day. I only received eight birthday cards, but it's still a great day.

When I think of all the people on the outside who were my so - called friends. The people I hung out with and worshiped with, where are they on my birthday?

Thank you, God, for the eight cards. I do not want to seem ungrateful. In the first months of this incarceration, I received at least **80** cards and letters. I praise you for being faithful and the faithful few who have consistently written, sent cards and pictures. I especially thank you God for my baby sister, Cynthia from Ohio, who came to see me every other month. My Godson, Dedric would fly from Los Angela, California to my home in Georgia to handle my business and then drove two hours to see me at least once a month. He never dropped the ball.

Then I have a friend name Paula Cook who drove down on Super Bowl Sunday to spend a day of visitation with me. I'm thankful for Cynthia's children and my three other friends up north Crystal Smith, Michelle Horton, and Phyllis Autry who were trying. They sent money, books and a letter or a card on a few occasions. I realize people have lives and their world does not revolve around me, although I did think it did at one time. Lol.

I know it's difficult for everyone; my mom, husband, child, friends and colleagues. None of my real friends and family understands how God allowed this to be.

But... I continued to point them back to God's purpose. I tell myself, it's just a test and I'm honored God chose me, but it's still hard. My family and friends are making real sacrifices flying to see me and taking care of my personal businesses. I can't take them for granted. So many ladies in here have family members who couldn't care less, or just burnt out because of their "revolving door" and extended stays of incarceration. I'm so blessed and thankful to God for my friends and family.

Then I think of the scripture, "Have you considered my servant Job?" However, it's not Job that's being tested, it's Edith? Now my flesh doesn't like it, but flesh is what's supposed to be dead, mortified, and crucified being tried in the furnace of affliction, right? Flesh, it's supposed to be burned up, the dross burned off, all the chaff blown away with the wind of adversity. This is so the real Edith can come out as pure gold.

This is my prayer, Lord:

"Thank you, Jesus, for my growth, maturity and real deliverance. Another year older tomorrow, both naturally and supernaturally.

Father, continue to uphold me with your right hand of righteousness and work on me with your left hand behind the scenes. Amen"

January 7, 2017 - Happy Birthday To Me. I'm 57 years young!

It was my birthday and I looked over my life and realized I had so much to be thankful for. This situation was a temporary road block to something good God has for me. **I feel it**. Like other people in the bible, we must all go through trials and tribulations. What is my true test, lord? I am here between these four walls trying to understand. Then, the story of Joseph comes to mind at this time. Joseph was thrown into prison and accused of something he didn't do.

However, how that story ends had such an impact on his family and the world overall. What is my story lord? What am I going to be used for?

It's my birthday and I thank you God for so many things!

Thank you for another day to serve you.

Thank you for the present of your divine presence.

Thank you for the grace to endure at Emmanuel Women Facility.

Thank you for enlightening my understanding.

Thank you for showing me where I really am in you.

Thank you for showing divine favor with you and man.

Thank you for wisdom, knowledge and understanding.

Thank you for breaking, making and molding me.

Thank you for this furnace of affliction while in prison.

Thank you for the pruning and chastisement.

Thank you for the washing and cleansing in the word.

Thank you for bottling up every one of my tears.

Thank you for divine calibration and resetting my steps.

Thank you for a complete overhaul and alignment.

Thank you for creating a clean heart and renewing a right spirit.

Thank you for peace that surpasses my understanding.

Thank you for joy, unspeakable and full of glory.

Thank you for the blessing through the pressing.

Thank you for the revelation of your word in me.

Thank you for the will to do of your good pleasure.

Thank you for the love of you in me toward others.

Thank you for the journey with all of its hurdles and curves.

Thank you for the strength, patience and the Holy Spirit inside.

Thank you for showing concern toward all that concerns me.

Thank you for your faithfulness and the faithfulness of family.

Thank you for real Friends and showing me those that are **not.**

Thank you for the resting, testing and questing.

Thank you for the Mountain top and the valley experiences.

Thank you for the strength to endure hardness as a good solider.

Thank you for the problems and the promise.

Thank you for the process and the provisions.

Thank you for the walk I have with you.

Thank you for your goodness and mercy all the days of my life.

This is a HAPPY, HAPPY, HAPPY BIRTHDAY FOR ME!

January 8, 2017 – "Bless The Lord O' My Soul and for All That Is Within Me. Bless His Holy Name."

Even though I remain here inside these walls, my birthday was so blessed. Dedric surprised me and showed up around 1:00 p.m. It made me so happy. Over the course of the three-hour visitation, I ate from the vending machine two sweet strawberry cream cheese pie slices, one cheese burger, chips, a ham and cheese sandwich, two small pan pizzas and a Sprite.

Free World Food, as we call it in here, is one of the highlights of visitation. It is food out of the vendor machine. It's still good because you can only have it during visitation. So, if your family comes in with a roll of quarters, that's golden. Actually, it was great seeing Dedric and we talked about relevant information. It had been three weeks since we'd even spoke. He's been on "Gale time" in California since December 10. Gale is Dedric's significant other. He takes her calls regardless to who he's with and what he is doing.

My fellow roommates and people in Room 5 made me nice cards with all the roomies signatures including women from Dorm H-2 and H-6. Ms. Nelson and Ms. Giles made me nice individual cards.

Free Indeed, a faithful ministry to the prison, came to minister to us and I received a free autograph book because it was my birthday. The church sang happy birthday and it felt great. I enjoyed Jesus, food, family and e-mails from my baby sister. I put cards on the wall by my bed, a dozen wonderful cards and kept them posted all weekend. I enjoyed looking at them, hallelujah! No inspection on the weekend.

Last night, I completed the Jericho walk! The 7thday of the 1st month, and 7 times around on the 7thday, the year of Jubilee for me; a trinity of 777. We walked around the gym (circle) the Jericho walk one time the first day, two times the second day etc. until you've walked seven days, seven times on the 7th day.

January 9, 2017 – Happy Birthday, Cynthia, my baby sis! I love you so much!

I made her a beautiful handkerchief with a poem that spelled out her name. I'm sure she's going to love it. I speak life, a long prosperous and healthy and happy life to Cynthia and her seeds. **Proverbs 18:21 – "Death and Life is in the power of the tongue...**

Matthew 6:33 says seek ye first the kingdom of God and all his righteous, then everything else will be added. The Lord has provided so I need not take any thought for the day – My God is sufficient. Radical for Christ class began today. Ten of us regulars attended with two new inmates.

7:30 a.m. - 9:00 a.m. – This was our time for class. It's always good to jump start the day with Jesus. I'm really enjoying listening to Smokey Norful music on my player all day long. His songs, "Communion Melody" takes me back to church. I sometimes get lost in my mind and forget where I am. I felt like I was in a place of peace.

Another song I love is the Medley of the Blood. Oh, the blood, there's power in the blood, nothing but the blood of Jesus, and Oh, how precious is the flow, all four of these songs. It's awesome, all eight minutes and 37 seconds...so enjoyable.

January 10, 2017 – It's my television day and I am going to watch it. We rotate duties in the room and only once a month do I watch whatever I want on television. I look forward to this of course. Game show Family Feud, Being Mary Jane, and Greenleaf are the only shows I wanted to see. Otherwise, TV was time wasted for me. When I did watch TV, it was very early morning on weekends Dr. Charles Stanley, Franklin Jensen, T.D. Jakes and of course my pastor, Bishop Dale C. Bronner of Word of Faith Family Worship Cathedral.

Tonight, the President of the United States Barak Obama will be giving his Fare Well speech at 8:00 p.m. tonight. Then Gabrielle Union, she's my favorite actress (being Mary Jane) at 10:00 p.m. I have not read my bible today, oops not good. But I am not going to beat myself up about it. God and I have an understanding. Lol.

I've had my last day of Re-Entry Class and have received my certificate. Hopefully, my case plan will be closed and I'm rolling out of here sooner than later. This day went by quickly; I rested, ate, relaxed, and watched TV. This is one day of the month that's mine and I'm taking it!

January 11, 2017 - I went walking outside. The weather was excellent. It was 9:00 a.m. It's been a great day. The weekly inmate Kairos class meets tonight at 7:00 p.m. I'm looking forward to that. I continued to walk my daily routine. As I was walking, my thought was on my family, friends, church and business. The freedom of walking gave me a sense of comfort. I also found myself talking with God as I looked up at the clouds. I could speed walk from the time they let us out on the yard until they called us to come back inside. Sometimes only one hour, sometimes two. It depended on the guard on duty. Today, I was led to the corner of the yard and prayed aloud in my heavenly language to God until He released me.

January 12, 2017 – I slept most of the day –There was no hot water so I had to Bird Bath in the sink. Of course these young smart-ass girls had something to say about nothing.   I kept my ear phones on all day. Sometimes the devil got in me and I wanted to knock some of these silly females on their butts! So, I did my best to keep studying, kept my earbuds plugged in listening to music or slept.

I'm spending my last waking hours writing notes for my up-coming class this weekend. This class was entitled, "Overcoming Adversity." As I've mentioned earlier, my friend Sharon Beaner and her husband David have a ministry called, Seeds of Love. She mailed me a very nice packet of what they had written about overcoming adversity. It consisted of twelve pages. I took this information and tailored it for the females in the prison.

Fifteen women signed up to take the class I taught for thirteen weeks.   It was all good. It was a powerful 90minute session held every Saturday and Sunday.

We also had anointed church services. I along with three or four other ministers, yes, ordained ministers, were locked up with me. They taught the gospel, on some of those Saturday nights. Is this the reason I'm here lord? I remember one night in the service; God spoke through me in an unknown tongue with the interpretation. This was talked about throughout the prison for a while. One girl named Dakota said, "Wow, I've never experienced anything like that in my whole life." God showed himself strong as many wept at the alter in repentance.

January 13, 2017 – So what if it's Friday the 13th? God is still on the throne. **"It is a day that the Lord has made; I will rejoice and be glad in it!"** I'm looking forward to seeing my mom on video visitation tonight at 5:00 p.m.

I love what I am hearing in my ear buds. Its Holy Ghost filled music that floods my soul all day. I wish I could just go around all day 24/7 without conversation and just listen to my music. Of course, that's not reality here. But I look for it to be like this in heaven when the time comes.

I would like to just do my work, eat, study, read, exercise and do Jesus-all day. Well, when I get to heaven, Jesus is exactly what I'll be doing all day. Now I understand why heaven will be so wonderful. Nothing but worship and praising God all day and night. Ok, back to reality.

EWF, Emmanuel Women's Facility, had an audit completed and they scored 100% in every department. So, the Warden decided to reward every offender with popcorn, candy bars and coke. This is something that's usually only offered on Fridays to the Dorm of the week, Wow! Of course, I took advantage of this day!

Everyone is excited for this treat. I played Backgammon/Acey-Ducie with Shavonne Giles until Chief Counselor Watkins called us out for a ministry team meeting.

It was good! Anybody in ministry knows how leadership meetings can be. Just like the church, there are pros and cons to "preachers." Yep, even in prison, some wanted to be identified as big I and little you. The Chief laid down the rules as to who will be doing what, rotation of schedules and appointed different ones to do different things. Pray, read scripture, words of encouragement, and preach.

I guess I will write some letters and thank you e-mails to those who remembered my birthday. One week ago, 57 years young, and still going strong in spite of my location.

"I believe you can bloom where ever you're planted and be a shining light in darkness as long as God is with you" is a statement my pastor, Bishop Dale C. Bronner preached one day at my church in Atlanta. I'm in the prison right now and Lord, I am learning and blooming. As long as I'm in him and he is in me. I'm good!

Now, my thoughts were on the words of my pastor during this time. It gave me strength and comfort. All the sermons over the years seem to give me strength to go on. It is funny how at different times when things were going on, another sermon would come to mind? Thank God I listened to his sermons diligently. (But I'm still in awe of my location). I know God knows what's best for me. This is a test of my faith. Am I passing the test Lord?

Saturday, January 14, 2017 – I woke up with the spirit of God all over me. Well, I guess he should be, since he lives on the inside. I'm so excited about facilitating my class today. Great breakfast! We had pancakes, syrup, sausage and eggs. There was no lunch on the weekends, Fridays, Saturdays and Sundays. You had to fend for yourself. My locker stayed loaded. I found myself sharing all the time.

I set up for visitation and went back to the Dorm H-8. I am enjoying Jesus in my ears. As I've said before, I wish I could keep ear buds in my ears 24/7. Then I would have Jesus all day long. I believe God chose me to overcome this adversity so I could teach others how to do it. The walk on the yard for 90 minutes was wonderful. Talking about Jesus with my sister in Christ Brunette Nelson, listening to music and the word all day is heavenly. I'm so glad I know that all I go through is not in vain. It's God's providential plan and purpose. It is well.

What if I didn't have God? How different would my life be? Would I be able to endure what is taking place in these walls? There were lesbians, fights, arguments, thieves, a few mean, unhappy and evil officers. I must say there were many very nice officers. My favorite officers were Lieutenant Hayes, Sergeant Lundy, Officer Poland, Officer Batty, and Officer Holland. All the counselors and 99 percent of the staff were very nice to me.

My husband has scheduled a video visit with me today at 5:00 p.m. I looked forward to hearing his progress. My husband was sentenced to six months of incarceration because he was married to me and was considered a "business partner". My husband gained almost 100 pounds in Johnson State prison. He was supposed to have a hip replacement in May. However, he went to prison in April instead and could not have it done as scheduled.

They said he could not have a cane or walker because it could be used as a weapon. So, they put him in a wheel chair. He sat, ate and got depressed over those six months. When my brother picked him up and took a selfie that was sent to me, my husband looked like a giant. He was already a big guy; but now his face and neck looked huge. He looked swollen and just wasn't doing well at all. I wasn't told the details of his plight until recently upon my release. It was an early ministry on TV in the a.m. while others were sleeping. I had just set up for visitation when I saw an old familiar message being taught by Dr. Tony Evans, who's a pastor in Texas. He leads the Urban Alternative Ministry. Dr. Evans said, **"There is a sure way to know if a detour in your life is from God."** There are four main points. This allowed me to see something Bishop Bonner taught his congregation once. He said, **"God is more concerned with developing your character than your comfort."**

Below are the four points that were delivered by Dr. Evans:

1. Being persecuted for righteousness sake.
2. God shows you his presence twice in the midst of the persecution.
3. God gives you people to serve while in this situation. You comfort others while you need comfort for yourself.
4. God prolongs your release."

January 15, 2017 - Dr. Tony Evans message was "**The Proof of Detours" – Is this from God?"**

Below are my notes from his message. Is this truly a message from God to help and comfort me while on this journey? Review these points and see for yourself how they apply to me. I am only an example to show others how to do it.

"Being persecuted for righteousness." – Accused for something you didn't do. This was a double blessing for Joseph, am I being tested due to my commitment to God? **1 Peter 2:20 says "For what credit is it if, when you are beaten for your faults, you take it patiently, but when you do good and suffer, if you take it patiently, this is commendable before God."**

God, I am trying to obey your word and the lesson you are teaching me between these walls. Help me to remain patient Lord. Amen

"God shows you his presence in the midst of your persecution" – God went into the furnace with Shadrach, Meshach and Abednego. The lord was also with Joseph. Because the Lord was with Joseph, he was promoted in jail and you know the rest of that story. If you don't know it, read **Genesis 39:22.**

Shadrach, Meshach and Abednego refused to bow down to the king's image. They are thrown into the furnace but God preserves them from harm and the king sees four men walking in the furnace, **Daniel 3:25.**

These stories tell us that God is always with us even when we question where he is during our storms.

God showed up in Joseph's life two times. (1) Joseph becomes the head of Potiphar's house and (2) when he became the captain of the guard in prison **Genesis 39:5; Genesis 39:22.**

Even after Joseph's release, he then became the head of Pharaoh's land **(Genesis 41:40).**

"God gives you people to serve while you're suffering." There were two guys put in prison with Joseph. He served them while he was a prisoner too. **Verse 20** – Pharaoh's Birthday. He had a baker, and a cup bearer, to taste food and drinks at his birthday party – two criminals held a key to Joseph destiny. Joseph asked them both **"why are your faces so sad?"** Joseph's gift was being a dreamer and interpreter of dreams. God is saying; help someone with their dream until it's your turn.

Just use your gifts to help others. God says, **"Comfort others when you need comfort."**

When God postpone your release. God gave the baker three days to prepare to die. He would not have had these three days to prepare had Joseph not interpreted his dream.

Here Joseph is kidnapped from his Hebrew land and didn't even belong in prison, like me. But God used him just as he's using me.

Joseph said to the butler, **"now that I've helped you, help me. Go tell Pharaoh I didn't do it, Verse 23.** But the Chief Cup Bearer forgot Joseph for two years.

Genesis 41:1 and Verse 9 - What do you do when you think God's forgotten you? Joseph spent two more years in prison. It looked like he was forgotten. But God has not forgotten me. The book "Life's Detours" by Dr. Tony Evans reminded me of this. God will give you a promotion on your detour of destiny. God may disappoint you when you expect your release. But Edith, your release is coming.

Look at the disciples who were on the ship. "Lord save us, carest thou not that we perish"? **Matthew 8:25**.

When God goes left, it's actually good news. I can't take any credit for my deliverance. No hook up, no contacts, no self-sufficiency only God gets the credit. Only God.

January 16, 2017 – Happy Birthday – Dr. Martin Luther King.

I didn't get the opportunity to attend or watch the traditional Martin Luther King celebration. But I will forever hold the memories of all the historical speakers I've heard over the years. I'm now making memories and historical moment of my own. Lord, I continuously thank you for all things. In everything I give thanks. I know my being here is the will of God concerning me.

January 17, 2017 – Worship While I wait!

I spent this morning listening to the word of God on my player in the wee hours of the morning, reading the word of God, allowing it to marinate in my spirit.

Thank you, God, for favor with man. Officer Batty allowed me to go into the Gym to shower. The hot water here at Emmanuel Women's Facility is broken. We've all had to use the gym and the drama has been much. There are 150 females in H dorm with only 3 showers in the gym. I'm thankful and blessed to be able to keep my early morning 4:30 a.m. schedule which is the same time that I usually shower while most everyone is still sleeping. No one is causing me drama. Thank you, Jesus!

Breakfast was great. I've been outside and walked five miles. I came in and received all my store items. I also napped thirty minutes. I'm excited to be starting Pilates tonight at 5:15 – 6:00 p.m. But I've got choir rehearsal at 4:30 – 6:00 p.m. I guess I have to leave choir early. I am hoping to get some letters out in the a.m. I will be writing letters to Angela Moore, Crystal Smith and Minnie Daniels.

It's been a great day and I'm truly blessed to be at peace with what God is doing in my life.

I never thought I'd say this out loud, but I'm willing, not wanting to, but willing. I'm willing to do and to stay as long as he needs me to deliver his word.

January 18, 2018 p.m. – More Belated Birthday Cards.

This was unexpected. But Mom, Gwen, Dee, Minnie, Michele and Ms. Joyce Riley in Los, Angeles, California all sent me birthday cards. I'm so glad someone is thinking about me. Late is better than not at all, I'm grateful. Today was another blessed and relaxed day of writing for me.

January 19, 2017 – The Warden has called me and my roommate, Jessica, to come to her office. She wants to ask us about starting an Aerobic class. While sitting there, I felt peace and thought I was on the outside. I asked for candy on the table from the candy bowl next to me and also reached for one of her business cards sitting in front of me on her desk. I literally forgot where I was. The Warden starred at me like I was crazy and then she laughingly smiled telling me to put it back. On the outside, we'd be friends I thought to myself. I enjoyed a colleague connection. Lol.

January 20, 2017 – 9:00 a.m. - Prepared for class

Jessica and I taught Aerobics class from 9:30 – 10:30 a.m.– Wow! We taught the second class from 1:00 – 2:30 p.m. It was exhausting but so much fun. The Warden, Ms. McMillian, Chief Counselor Watkins and Caption Cody stayed and watched almost the entire time. It was the first Aerobics class in the prison and it was good. I then showered, groomed and dressed.   It was chow time. This day flew by.

January 21, 2017 – I'm up early and had breakfast.

I set up visitation details and then spent time studying my word until called out to participate in Kairos. Only a selected number of people were permitted to attend Kairos, based on criteria selected by Deputy Warden Hendrix. This was an awesome experience where a group of women from the outside showed the love of God to us with FULL COURSE MEALS; breakfast, lunch, and fresh homemade cookies. Kairos offered a lot of singing, readings, poems, ministry from ordained ministers and lay persons alike. We were allowed to participate in portions of the ministry.   I **quoted** the entire Psalms 27 verses 1-14 which encouraged people to study and learn their word as well.

My class started at 1:00 p.m. Thirteen participants arrived and we all had a good time. The name of the class was "Overcoming Adversity." I asked all the attendees the question, "What scripture have you located in your bible to overcome the adversity that you face?" There was 100% participation.

As soon as class was over, it's count time. Once count cleared, I went to visitation to break down the visitation seating and set up the tables and chairs for chow.

After dinner at 5:00 p.m., I needed a nap. There was a scheduled church service at 7:00 p.m. and Beaches, the new TV show with Nia Long, was to begin at 8:00 p.m. I knew I'd miss it if I went to church and was torn on what to do. Even though I love church and wanted to participate, I really wanted to watch the show. The movie Beaches with Barbra Hershey and Bette Midler is one of my favorites. This was a re-make of the original.

Unfortunately, I overslept and the guard had already done last call and I couldn't get out. So, I honestly missed going to the service. I missed church because I was so tired and really needed the rest. I slept until it as too late to go. Nevertheless, at 8:00 p.m., the new remake of Beaches came on and it was good, but not as good as the original. I went right back to sleep after it went off. I slept until morning, I was really tired.

January 29, 2017 – It's been a week since I've written in my journal.

I've been busy writing letters and e-mailing a dozen or so people in my supportive data base. I wrote Pat Bowen, a great friend, my sister, Cynthia and her daughter, Andrea in Ohio, Angela, my best friend, Dee Myers, Joyce Beeks, Michelle in Detroit, Dedric in California and of course my husband, Ozzie.

Ozzie and I don't have much to write to each other because I can call, video, and e-mail. Unfortunately, we don't have much to talk about on my face time either.

My marriage was on the rocks. In my mind, I had been divorcing him every other day of the week.

Nevertheless, I am going to stay on my face seeking God about what he wants from me in that department.

No church service today. But I can have "church" all by myself. I've been thinking about Ms. Joyce Riley in L.A., a friend and supporter of Dedric. She is a person I've never met. But because of her connection of love and trust for Dedric, I believe we are going to be good friends. I may even spend a summer in California, if God allows it! My mind says I need to work, save and build up money. I'm really going to try my best to rely on the Spirit of God to direct my path. I really don't want to get ahead of God or get in the way of what God wants to do in my life. While I want to make money and Nursing has always been my "back-up," I don't want to start doing my own thing and miss the opportunity God is setting me up for.

I came back to my bunk and started to journal again. Time flies when you're having fun. I can't believe I am saying this. Am I adjusting or accepting what God has put in front of me? I'm going to bed early tonight so I can get up early for aerobics in the morning.

January 30, 2017 – Radicals for Christ was great today! We discussed the love of God. We are studying **I Corinthians Chapter 18, John Chapter 3 and St. John 21:15-17, Peter...**Feed my sheep. Afterwards, I had lunch, rested, took another exercise class, made sure I was available for count time, and then showered. I'm repeating the same thing on a regular basis. I'm asking God to help me slow down wanting to do more and then to give me the wisdom and revelation of his word that he speaks.

January 31, 2017 – Scrabble class, going great and then I hear my name called out over the P.A., loud speaker, to report up front. Thirteen other names were called.

Its Warden McMillian letting us know that she personally handpicked us to be the first in the class called "Women of Empowerment" that she herself is teaching. I'm so excited. This will be a class where she will be giving us a certificate upon completion. This certificate will be placed with a note in scribe. Scribe is an internal computer program to the Parole Board. The class will be held every Monday and Wednesday at five o'clock until six thirty p.m. for six weeks starting Monday, February 6 and each Monday and Wednesday thereafter.

Its 3:50 a.m., I'm wide awake. Lord, you must want to speak. 4:00 a.m., I showered, groomed and read my bible.

I wrote a letter to Angela. Oh wow, I received an e-mail from Dedric today. Well, it's about 6:00 a.m., time to prepare to head over for breakfast. I'm so sleepy now. After a.m. count time and inspection, I then noted that I have an appointment for a physical at 8:40 a.m. Now I'm back in my dorm at 10:00 a.m. Wow, I've lost eight pounds in three weeks. I'm so motivated. I want to get on the treadmill for twenty minutes full speed and on high incline.

Now I'm hungry and ready for lunch. Its 3:00 p.m. and its count time. 4:00 p.m. I am eating dinner. Its 4:30 p.m. I am running to Choir Rehearsal, it's now 6:00 p.m. and Yard call takes place until 7:00 p.m.

I called Ozzie, no answer, and Cynthia at 7:10 p.m. I called Ozzie until 8:00 p.m. He's not there. When I did speak with him, he told me he had been out with my sister, Gwen, since 6:00 p.m. Of course, I told him about a text I received from Dedric. He was mad I heard from Dedric and accused me of listening and believing Dedric and the lies of the staff over him. Ozzie was "upset" that Dedric was still "in charge" of the business and he didn't feel comfortable in our own home. We had one tenant renting a part of the house with his care giver and Ozzie didn't feel "free" to do as he pleased in "our home." I didn't care how he felt, Dedric was in charge. In hind sight, (I was wrong) I was not being very nice to Ozzie.

CHAPTER 5
OVERCOMING ADVERSITIES!

February 1, 2017 – Finally, I received Ozzie's Probation Officer's letter of approval for his visitation privilege to come see me in prison. I was mad that he was out in only six month and I was still in for a three-year sentence. I put the letter in an envelope to Chief Counselor Watkins with an explanation and requested his visitation be approved.

Wow, time flies. Yesterday was my busiest day this entire week. I was up at 6:30 a.m. but missed breakfast. Oatmeal and Bran Flakes are not something I eat, so I didn't mind missing it. I slept till I had to get up for count. My cleaning and dusting duty that I'm assigned to do in the room is complete. Now it's time to go to the gym to set up for Aerobics. A full hour-work out and then I wrote e-mails until time for lunch. With only an hour left until time for the next Aerobics class at 1:00 p.m., I had to leave class to get an x-ray of my right knee.

I could not get on my right knee to pray at all. It became extremely painful overnight. At 2:00 p.m. I walked until time to come back in for 3:00 p.m. count. Once count cleared, it was time to prepare to go to dinner. After dinner in an hour, it's time to go to Intercessory prayer. It's 6:00 p.m. and I took a rest period and prayed. Now it is time for Kairos at 7:00 p.m. to 8:00 p.m.

Our floor is being waxed so I can't go into the dorm room. I called Dedric. He vented and complained about Ozzie regarding a number of things. I had to make three phone calls before he was calm. I then reached Cynthia and asked her if she'd be willing to make room for Ozzie in Toledo. Dedric did not like Ozzie and Ozzie felt disrespected by Dedric. Dedric said, Ozzie had to go or he was moving the renter out. Ozzie had nowhere to go. He and Dedric were just not going to be able to function in the same zip code. Ozzie had no family in Georgia and his sisters in Florida had families of their own. He really didn't want to entertain the idea of going to live with my family.

Later, Cynthia offered him a room in her home in Toledo. However, Ozzie learned that he could not leave the state of Georgia while on probation for at least 90 days upon his release. He'd need to speak to his Parole Officer today and get a "hardship" transfer to Ohio. He needs a plan to move. My husband is no longer comfortable nor is he wanted by the staff in our own home. I was having mixed feeling about remaining married to him and really didn't support him remaining in our home. Why was I angry with Ozzie? He was out after six months and here

I am still in, among other conflicts we were having before our incarceration.

After all the drama outside the prison with Ozzie and Dedric, I'm thankful to my friend Shavonne Giles. Since I couldn't get to my room, I played Backgammon and ate snacks she had in the Day room. I also watched Showtime at the Apollo, Stars and Vivica Fox Black Magic dancers.

After the floor was dry enough to go into the room with socks only, it was time to buff. This facility is serious about their floors. I was stuck in the dorm room on my bunk. I ate a snack and went to sleep at 11:30 p.m. This was a long day.

February 2, 2017 – Wow! This year is flying by. I'm asking God to teach me to number my days. It's going so fast. His return is much sooner than we think. It is wellness time and I am going walking outside. Ninety minutes of walking felt great. I showered, changed clothes and went to sleep. Lunch was not great – it was spaghetti, greens and fruit. What was I expecting? I am in prison. I came back to the room and made tuna with trail mix.

You might be wondering, do people take your food? No, I have a locker with a lock on it and that is where I keep my food and nobody bothers it. In fact, let me tell you something. In here, there is an unspoken rule that you do not ask people for their food. If you do, that means they will expect "something" from you. **If a female put a honey bun on your pillow, that meant she wanted you, and if you ate it, that meant you were hers. If you didn't flow like that, then you made a scene and threw the honey bun in the trash so everyone would know, you are not into that lifestyle.**

Anyway, after my home-made tuna lunch, I went to sleep and when I woke up, I realized I was going to be late for Scrabble class. So, I didn't go. I pulled out my player and e-mailed Dedric. Half-way through it, the prison called "online for inspection," so I'll have to finish this e-mail later... It's later and now my player is dead.

February 4, 2017 – Keeping this journal helps me stay sane. I missed writing yesterday, February 3, 2017. My purpose is to write something every day.   It's early Saturday morning and I'm going to be so busy today. I have to set up for Visitation at 6:30 a.m.

By the time I return to my dorm and read scripture, it's time for 9:30 to 10:30 Body Sculpture class. After class, I went back to the dorm to shower and its count time. About 11:00 a.m., I'll fix my lunch. Today I'm "cooking." Cooking consisted of using the outer paper wrap of the toilet paper to place your tortilla wraps stuffed with rice, cheese and whatever you wanted to put into it and place it in the flat irons to cook.

Now it's time for the class which I facilitate, "Overcoming Adversities" from 1:00 until 2:30 p.m. After 3:00 p.m. count, I go to breakdown visitation and set up for chow.

I ran back to the dorm to get my Spork (spoon and fork combined) and back in line for chow again. After eating, now I'm sleepy. If I lay down, I know I'm not going to get up when choir is called out for inmate service tonight. Sure enough, I lay down and didn't get back up until 6:50 p.m. Church service started at 7:00 p.m. I was a few minutes late, but ran to the chapel anyway. Once I got there, I jumped right on in with the praises and had a great time. I sang with the choir. However, half way through the message, I fell asleep. Tammy McMullen speaks in monotone and is very low key when preaching. So, I'm fighting to stay awake. When it was over, I went to the dorm to ice my right knee which feels like it's on fire and I'm going to bed with a Chocolate Hostess Cream filled cupcake tonight. Oh my! Good night.

February 5, 2017 - I'm definitely not going to Body Sculpturing work out class today. I'm exhausted and my right knee hurts. I went to the gym to tell Teresa, the instructor, and then I'm going back to bed. Of course, I still have to get up for count. I laid back down to listen to the audio scriptures on my player. I am awakened by my bunkie who informed me that I had a visitor. I'm shocked because I'm thinking it must be a holiday because Dedric surprised me for my birthday last month. Who could this be?

February 6, 2017 – Super bowl Sunday was nice. The best part was my friend Paula Cook came to see me on the biggest day of the season where most want to just eat, drink and be merry. I relaxed on this day with food and my friend. I had a good time. Paula drove two and a half hours and then had to drive back home those same two and a half hours. That's five hours of driving in a day and I am so appreciative of her sacrifice, and on such a special day. What a super friend on Super Sunday. I was so surprised and happy to see her yesterday.

Paula has so many great ideas and seeks to implement all kinds of business adventures. She already has tenants who rent from her. She's a hair stylist, she has hospitals biding for her to come and work for them, and she has her own whole life projects to master. So, I don't think she's going to be on anyone's scheduled "job" any length of time. Paula is one of a kind and a champion in her own way. She has so many plans for a great future. I'm pleased to call her my friend.

God has given her a vision for a new clothing line of sexy t-shirts with great saying to back them up. The t-shirts show her skills, she has a tee-shirt line called; MY HAIR

SPEAKS with sayings like, "curls have more fun" and "Shushhhh... my hair is speaking." Paula is an author, a hair stylist, a public speaker, cook, caterer, trainer, runner and all-around entrepreneur with her Whole Life Project. I can't wait to get out and team up with her. We took pictures together before she left. Yes, another fantastic privilege of this prison. An inmate photographer, Ms. Nelson.

Tonight, I received mail from my ex-sister in law, Karol Cook, with a heartfelt sincere message of importance. I'm glad to hear her good news and to know that she is doing so much better. My mom also sent a card. I will write both of them back tomorrow. Good night.

February 7, 2017 - Its 9:30 a.m. and I am sitting on my bunk. I'm cleaning out an envelope of stuff that just needs to be done. I'm pleased I got three letters out this morning. I was up at 2:00 a.m. completing letters to my brother Tim, Minnie Daniels and my best friend forever (BFF), Angela Moore. I received an e-mail from my baby sister, Cynthia, letting me know that mom put a hundred dollars in the prison bank and she sent my package order form to Pat Bowen. Pat sent me books on a regular base to keep me entertained, a series of novels that I thoroughly enjoyed.

March will be here before we know it. I'm so glad time is flying quickly. I was so happy to receive a letter from

Karol Cook, my ex-sister in law, the mother to my brother James three children. I'm going to pray and seek the guidance as to what I'm to say in my return letter to Karol. The only order of business I have today is to write letters, clean out my locker, make my bed, eat lunch and play Scrabble at 1:00 p.m. I will walk the yard at 2:00 p.m. and then nap. At 3:00 p.m. there is count. After dinner I've got choir rehearsal.

After rehearsal, Giles cooked us a good snack and I'm in for the night. How did we cook in prison, not just the microwave? We cooked food with flat irons. You can become really innovated while in prison. There are so many talents and gifts that are all locked up. I wish I could show the talents of braiding hair, art work and, making all kinds of things out of nothing. And the hair styles, OMG, you've not seen braids until you've seen prison braids. Empty little Debbie cake boxes become journal covers and birthday cards. One man's "trash," gum wrappers, scraps of anything can become the masterpiece of a talented inmate one example would be Brittany's Bags.

I wish I had a picture of the gorgeous handbags she made with gum wrappers. I told her she need her own boutique

I just got mail from Tahiem Nipper and Joyce Reiley in LA. What a pleasant surprise. I'm absolutely going to take the rest of this night to write them back.

February 8, 2017 – I'm up for breakfast. We had sausage, grits and coffee cakes. It's exercise day at 10:30 a.m. and 1:00 p.m. I'm supposed to have a class with the warden. The name of this class is "Women of Empowerment." But, I'm on the schedule for a Perm. My hair certainly takes priority today. Yes, there is a salon in prison with a licensed instructor that supervises ladies who are working on their cosmetology license. You can become educated, skilled and licensed in prison. For those who need or want an education, there is no excuse for these females not to come out "better."

My day is full, but I'm making time to study my word and seek the Lord for some more directions in his word. I'm committed to obeying God all the way live.

My hair turned out beautifully and I'm sure the lord is pleased. Lol... The Warden's class, I'm told, was very interesting. I'm going to get the notes and work on whatever it is I need to do for next week. Until then, I'm making my good friend some food. I'm grateful to God everything is well as it is. I will not complain about a thing.

I'm so interested in digging deeper into God's word according to the scripture, to search out words like, straightway, immediately and suddenly……. spending time in the word and in his presence. God, you are so good to me!

February 11, 2017 – I'm spending time in God's word. I truly enjoy the study of God's word. <u>There's nothing better than being in the presence of the Lord</u>. God's knowledge and wisdom, his instruction to lead me always leads to the best for me. I'm consistently and persistently seeking God for direction and instructions for me. Overcoming Adversities is the class I'm facilitating and the future of God's perfect will is resting with me at this season in my life.

One thing I'm hearing in my Spirit is to write out scenarios for each student to answer by the end of the next class. The questions must be answered using scriptures only. It must offer the answer to the adversity. Here are the directions:

Give **three scriptures** for **(1) breakfast, (2) lunch and (3) dinner** that you would use to comfort this person. How would you respond correctly with the Scriptures when these following statements are made?

- My doctor has diagnosed me with cancer OMG, (Oh My God). I'm so scared...
- My newborn has been diagnosed with Down syndrome. God Why?

- My fiancé was killed in a plane crash a month before our wedding and I'm pregnant. What am I going to do?
- A tornado ripped through my town and everything is gone. My insurance won't pay anything because it was an act of God. Now, God, why and what are you going to do – why me?
- I've been sentenced to ten years in prison, I've got the class writing out their own adversity and those sceneries that are potentially their own adversities. What scripture can you come up with that can be used to comfort others. Note: This assignment will cause each student to search out the word for themselves. No more spoon feeding them.

February 12, 2017 – Pray Until You Get Your **Sugar!**

This came from my brother in California. **Tim's Nym's** he calls it. This is his gift and this is his <u>copy *written information, used by permission of course.*</u>

Speak and keep on speaking

Until faith becomes strong and

God gives you the assurance and

Answers you according to his word

Revealing the final manifestation to his word.

Scriptural steps to get your **SUGAR.**

1. Find scripture that supports what you believe God for:

- **Isaiah 43:26,**

- **I John 5:14-15**

- **Daniel 9:2**

- **II Corinthians 4:13.**

- Do three things daily with God's word. **Speak** it, **meditate** on it and **obey it.**

- **Joshua 1:8**

- **Psalms 1: 1-6**

- **Luke 18:8**

- Speak only what you truly believe and keep on speaking it aloud until you get the victory.

- **II Corinthians 4:13**

- **James 1:5-8**

- **Numbers 14:28**

- Be persistent until you get what you're after and resists all obstacles of your faith to doubt.

- **Acts 12: 1-17**

- Luke 18: 1-8

- Mark 11:22-24

- Don't stop speaking until you have the final fruit of the substance that you're after.

- Acts 12: 1-17

- Luke 1: 42-45

- Hebrew 11: 1-3, 6

Here's another way to hit your **TARGET!**

Take legal **A**uthority in the **R**ealm of the spirit and **G**ain the necessary ground by **E**ngaging the specific circumstances **through** targeting specific problems with scriptures that always hit their mark!

The only way to always consistently hit your mark is to take the necessary time to advance in prayer. You may often hear people complaining about various issues or problems. But God has instructed us to speak the solutions and not the problem that you see.

Proof is in the prophet **Elisha** in **I King 17:20** where he prayed the problem and nothing happened, then in **I Kings 17:21** the prophet tried a different approach. He prayed the solution and obtained results.

February 13, 2017 – What a way to start my Monday morning for the week. Radicals for Christ 7:30 a.m.

Prayer/Worship and then studying the word of God with fellow believers. I won't share the notes as this class material was taught by Pastor Brunette Nelson. Although it's the word of God, which belongs to us all, I

do not want to appear as if it's "my work." I will say that the discussion was about Rest, Restoration and Reconciliation. She spoke about the relationship between Peter and Jesus. The homework question was what are the center, character, contribution, community and communication of your life?

Scripture References were: **Act 13:36**

I John 13-17,   **II Corinthians 14:4 and 4:17**

Galatians 5:22-26   **Psalms 4:26**

Ephesians 3:17   **Philippians**
1: 10, 4: 7-11

Revelations 4:11   **Esther 4:14**

February 16, 2017 – It's Thursday and I didn't journal Tuesday or Wednesday. I guess I've spent so much time reading, studying my word and preparing for class notes. All my writing went into class work. Today, I went on a spell of writing early this am and got two letters in the mail at breakfast time. I then came back to the dorm until it was time to leave for my 9:00 a.m. Wellness walk. I'm now emailing and remembered I have to drink a gallon of Go lightly to prep for a colonoscopy. Then I heard the call for Scrabble Class. Of course, I have to go. But I really didn't want to. It's not always a very pleasant atmosphere. In fact, that was the beginning of my downhill today. Silly, young, child-like adults got on my nerves. I left the Scrabble table and went to tell my counselor, I quit! She wouldn't let me quit so I went back to the group like a big girl and worked it out.

Then I went to my appointment. Between the foolishness of the girls and drinking that lemon-flavored salt water, I'm finally empty. I hurried back to my dorm.

Before I can get to my room, I'm told by an inmate to get in line for a meeting with Ms. Wadley in the gym about voting for a dorm rep and meeting with facilitators regarding their classes. It was a train wreck. I will be glad to get out of here away from all this foolishness. I just can't do this anymore, grown silly women fussing about nothing and complaining about everything. "Father, help me and Jesus take the wheel". It's the climb by Miley Cyrus kicked in my Spirit. Ok Jesus, help me climb.

February 18, 2017 – Kairos today. All day 7:00 a.m. – 3:00 p.m. It's going to be exciting **Retreat talks and discussions.** This was truly a very powerful experience. There were special songs and prayers presented. We were "served" like queens, enveloped in unconditional love, feasted naturally and spiritually and just soaked in the presence of the Holy Spirit ALL DAY.

After a discussion and talks with Kairos today and eating a lot of pizza, I'm stuffed and ready to sleep. However, as soon as count clears, I'm summoned to break down visitation. I'm too full to eat, so I go to dinner just to give my tray away to a roomie who doesn't make store and will enjoy eating this meal today.

Once I get back to lie down, I can't sleep. There's a good movie on that I watched. Now, someone's at the door for me. A student from my "Overcoming Adversities" class came to me after class for the scriptures she needed. It's now time to get ready for church.

I'm wondering what I'm going to speak on tonight? I certainly don't have to wonder what I'm going to wear. Lol.

I was called out early for practice with the choir and I pulled a sermon out of my folder of my many messages. "Everybody Talk'n about Heaven Ain't Going There!" This is not a popular topic because people want to do what they want to do, sin. They think it's going to just be overlooked by our heavenly father. Not! People want somebody to just preach them into heaven – not so! If nobody claps or says, amen, I'm going to deliver the unadulterated word of God no matter who doesn't like it.

I know when I obey God, he will prevail. Just like Daniel, as he acknowledged God as the one and only God who reveal secrets. **Daniel 2:28**. Daniel says only what God has shown him. Then it is the power of God who caused the King in Verse 46 and 47 to say that Daniels God is the God of Gods, a Lord of kings, and a revealer of secrets of which then proved God; causing the king to make Daniel a great man giving him great gifts, and setting Daniel up as a ruler over the providence of Babylon. Yes Lord, there is a God in heaven. Hallelujah.

February 19, 2017 – Of course routine hasn't changed. Up at breakfast then set up for visitation. Then I went to the gym for "Body Sculpture" class. I came back and showered, dressed, read and prayed.

After 11:00 a.m. count, detail, chow, and it's almost time for my class at 1:00 p.m. Now, let's see what God does with all the opposition coming against this class, "Overcoming Adversities."

The devil is mad and is even getting in two of the thirteen students trying to show discord. But the devil is a liar and we are shutting him down!

There were only ten of us in class today and there was a great anointing and powerful teaching. Even with only a few of us, it was a time of caring and sharing allowing God to have his way. Those students that missed class, missed God, that's all I can say. We prayed out and left. Walking down the corridor across the breezeway when I saw in a distance the three who missed class, my flesh wanted to confront them. I was able to not even say a word.

Later, I saw one of them alone who'd been "broken," crying because a so-called best friend "let her down." Of course, I prayed for her. The other two who'd missed class tried to avoid eye contact with me because they knew they were wrong. I thought to myself, O well, their loss. I'll continue to pray for them and continued without saying a word to either of the two. I was able to nap and later ate a snack. I didn't attend Free Indeed

Church service this night. I just rested in the presence of the Lord. God is so good to me and I love him so much.

February 20, 2017 – I got up at 4:45 a.m. showered, dressed, and journaled and read the book of Daniel. I'll try to complete one more letter as I wait to go to breakfast.

February 21, 2017 4:00 a.m. – My friend, Brunetta Nelson has been transferred to the Transitional Center this morning. While I'm sad and will miss her dearly, I'm happy for her. Breakfast wasn't the same. Although she rarely went to breakfast, it's still strange that she's not going to be in the Day room to talk. Let me stop. I am starting to cry again. Well, I've still got Giles, my other sister in Christ. It's not the same. Giles is our Choir Director. She loves the word, but she's a laid-back Christian, not visibly spiritual like Nelson. But it's ok. I still love her too, just differently.

I'm done with my detail, reading the bible and need to get ready to go out on my Wellness walk. I'm use to walking fast and no one walks as fast as I do. I couldn't even walk my normal fast speed today. I'm more like sulking and missing my friend. I'm going to sit down and listen to my music something I never do outside. I was called into medical. I sat two hours for the doctor to tell me what I already knew. My colonoscopy was normal and I needed to have it done again in ten years. When I left the hospital on the 19th, they gave me these results in writing. Anyway, I'm back to my bunk, not wanting to talk to anyone. I know I'm wearing my feeling on my face. One of the students came to get me following afternoon count, trying to cheer me up.

February 22, 2017 – My students went over the class notes she's recopied from me and we discussed it. I did feel a little better after dinner. I sat and e-mailed my sister, Cynthia, who told me that Eterica Maddox sent a message that "Nelson made it to the Transition center with her and they both missed me and loved me very much." I started to cry again. Wednesday is better. I'm not at my best. I'm sleepy and reflecting more than anything else.

My attendance in the Warden's class "Women Empowerment" helped. There was one antagonizing female, Celeste, who was so ghetto and only God can teach me how to love her.

February 23, 2017 – Today, I'm much better. God has truly helped me through this. I was able to muster up a smile this morning. I've walked several miles, ate and fellowshipped with others. I was so tired from being so busy. I fell asleep during choir rehearsal. I later received e-mail from my Godson from the Grand Canyon as well as a picture from him baking French bread. He is happy and is actually enjoying his life with Gale. So, I'm very happy for him.

Store order sheets just arrived and I'm going to only purchase Tuna, Mayo and pickles to make lunches for the week. I've got to lose weight so I'm going to only order a few sweets, one bag of chips, and just a few personal items, not a whole lot. It's actually a good day. Thank you, Lord.

February 24, 2017 - Today, I feel so inspired. I'm writing letters to my friend Phyllis Autry in Toledo, Ohio, Dee Myers in Georgia and Paula Cook in Jonesboro, Georgia. I'm also reading a book called "Necessary Endings" which is helping me to make some personal decisions in my life.

After reading a letter I received from my new associate in L.A. California Joyce Reily, I'm really thinking about the choice I've made in my past and what I need to do about it now for my future.

First and foremost, I'm still going to trust God at his word. **Proverbs 3:5-6 says "Trust in the word with all your heart. Lean not on your own understanding."** Allowing God to do it is the key! I must acknowledge him in all my ways and allow him to direct my path. I need to be obedient in what he says and not what I feel is the other key. Then **Colossians 1: 9-10** is what I've got to do. **"Be filled with the knowledge of his will"** in all wisdom and spiritual understanding. That ye might walk worthy of the lord unto all pleasing being fruitful in every good work and increasing in the knowledge of God." God is Sovereign. All his proverbial ruling will prevail no matter what. To make it smoother for me, I'm going to just choose to obey God the first time.

Yea and Amen! I am glad to be spending quality time reading this morning.

February 25, 2017 – This has been a great day. Breakfast was good. I had plenty of help setting up visitation, had a great workout on the treadmill and lunch was filling. Class today was "moving" and God is going to heal for so many. We read the divine books of **Jonah**, four short chapters, learning to cry out to God in the belly of the whale **Chapter 2.** Once you lament, supplicate and get down to business, God is going to move!

We should learn to just obey God the first time! I'm not even hungry. I'm ready to turn down my plate and just go all the way in and praise God until I pass out.

In my mind I'm thinking, now that I've declared Jesus is Lord and I'm in his will, I know I should expect that slew footed devil to show up. Nevertheless, when he does; I'm armed and ready with the word of God to slap him down to the ground under my foot where he belongs. Because I know the devil is such a crafty deceiver; that's one of the reasons I sometimes think out loud and speak words aloud as I know WORDS have power.

The service tonight was awesome as God had his way. People were hurting inside and I only know one sure way to handle the pain, Jesus Christ. Christ at the cross is still the answer! Pointing people to Jesus is my goal!

February 26, 2017 – This month is almost over. "Time waits for no man." Jesus is soon to come. All the signs of the times are here. **Genesis** reveals it all and all I can tell a person is "Get your house in order," he's coming again soon.

I have been here in H-dorm two months now. Lord, what is the reason for my being here? So far, I've taught classes, sang in the choir, listened to the word more than I ever have, been given the opportunity to teach and learned new skills. What will the month of March bring?

CHAPTER 6
IT'S NOT IN VAIN!

March 1, 2017 – "Bless the Lord oh my soul and all that is within me bless his holy name. Bless the Lord oh my soul and forget not all his benefits." OMG, I'm feeling impressed by the Lord to seek him, draw closer to him even more. Fasting and praying, less distractions, less talking to anybody—Reading, studying and meditating in the word lament and supplicate to God!

After my first day back to Aerobics class and being off sick Valentine's Day, I had two week's leave because of my right knee. I had tendonitis. I'm exercising some, but no jumping jacks. At 2:00 p.m., no one showed up for Aerobics class. So, I walked the treadmill a few minutes and then of course went into the room to rest, until time for the Wardens class.

At the end of the Warden's class, I went into the "Intercessory Prayer" group and God is drawing me. Father, help me to obey and fast, is my prayer. Jesus, take the wheel. **"This is the day you have made. I will rejoice and be glad in it."** I'm feeling like I need to spend quiet time with my face to the wall to simply hear from you. I have ear plugs in while I listen to music and the word of God on my player. It is yea and Amen all day long.

March 2, 2017 – I'm anxious for nothing. With prayer and supplication, I'm making my request made known unto God. Today I'm walking on the yard four to five miles a day, rest, lunch and playing Scrabble with the Scrabble club. I feel like the days are flying by. Tammi McMullan asked me to give words of encouragement for this Saturday night service. God lead me to what you would have me to say.

This is the weekend I will be speaking. I need to fast Friday, Saturday and Sunday, only liquids, water and broth. Oh, I forgot to mention some of the ladies on the dorm hall started the Jericho walk again last night on March 1, 2017. One lap each night until day seven which is the night, we will walk seven laps, blow the horn and believe God for Spiritual walls to fall down. For tonight's walk, I led the prayer. Now I know it's time to fast and pray. Beginning tomorrow, this is the weekend to turn down my plate. I've written e-mails to Ozzie keeping it real. Asking him to do what it takes to keep us together, the ball is in his court. Eighteen days from now will be our fifth year Wedding Anniversary. I sent e-mails to my nephew Kurtiss and my Godson Dedric. Now, I'll get into bed and allow God to prepare my heart for the weekend. Good night.

March 3, 2017 – I'm awake, listening to the noise of others getting up. I'm going to lay right here until everyone leaves the dorm to go to breakfast. Now I'm sponging off in the sink, groomed, dressed and made my bed. I'll get this day started in my word, prayer and feeding my spirit and starving my flesh! I declare in the name of Jesus that this day is totally blessed! This is the day that the Lord has made, **"I will rejoice and be glad in it."** Jesus, take the wheel.

7:00 a.m. - God's will, I'm spending time seeking the word he wants me to deliver for tomorrow night's inmate service.

Philippians 4:5 – "Let your moderation be known unto all men. The Lord is at hand!" Isaiah 55:6-7 – Seek ye the Lord, while he may be found, call upon him while he is near. Let the wicked forsake his way and the unrighteous man his thoughts and let him return unto the Lord and he will have mercy upon him and to our God, for he will abundantly pardon."

9:00 a.m. – Calling Wellness Walkers (announced over the P.A). I'm staying in for Aerobics at 9:30 - 10:30 a.m. Then I take a nap. I'm growing spiritually. The Christian life compared to a Foot race; Spiritually – Athletic – **I Corinthians 9:24. Galatians 5:7. Philippians 3:14, Hebrews 12:1, 2 Timothy 4:7, II Timothy 4:8 Spiritual Striving – Luke 13:24, I Corinthians 9:25, Philippians**

1:27 and that's the word of the Lord for the service tonight.

11:00 a.m. - It's count time – I just finished Aerobics and talking with Ms. Brantley. Upon my release, I'm excited because my sister, Cynthia and I will be hosting six of my officer and staff friends I've made here at EWF. **Ms. Brantley, Ms. Hill, Officer Poland and Holland, Sargent Lundy and Lt. Hayes** – All eight of us will travel together to a resort and have the best four-day weekend ever! My treat! – My desire is for us to fly out on Thursday night, check into our fabulous 5 Star Spa-hotel, spend Friday eating and shopping and maybe a live play late that evening. Saturday is Spa day and we get an all-day luxury deluxe manicure and pedicure, foot reflexology, facial, full body hot rock & oil massage, sauna, whirlpool, room service, relax and then special seating for fine dining at dinnertime. We will enjoy Sunday worship service, fellowship and fine dining again. Then we will relax at the pool and just enjoy one another's company. OK, back to today, (smile). I've got time for a nap while I wait for my 1:30 p.m. aerobics class.

Today is the first day of fasting this week. I am listening to music to keep me spiritually full now so I will not eat any popcorn. Jesus help! I'm not even hungry and I know that temptation can't even be bought to me today.

I must be steadfast unmovable, always abounding in the work of the Lord! My roomies are cooking in my room at the table directly across from my bed. But thank God, I have no temptation there. I don't like what their cooking. I also notice poor hand washing. If I wanted what they were eating, I've got all that in my locker to fix any time. So, praise God, devil, you can't use that.

March 4, 2017 – What a blessed day. Oh my God.   This is day two of my fast.   I'm having nothing but water, and it's not even a struggle. Thank you, Jesus. I'm feeding on the word of God all day and music by Smokie Norful, "The Communion Medley; the blood reaches to the highest mountain and flows to the lowest valley; there is power in the blood of the lamb, there is healing and joy. The blood will never lose its power; Oh the blood of Jesus. What can wash away my sins, nothing but the blood of Jesus." I love this entire medley of songs.

My room is in chaos, but it's just been a great day in his presence for me. I've been on the treadmill 50 minutes with worship songs in my ear – listening over and over – wow! I'm just enjoying the presence of the Lord. I will rest now, until it's time to go teach my class, God's class "Overcoming Adversities." I then return to my room to find a counselor talking to my roomie about a disturbance with Candice and Brock. I'm glad I was at my detail working. I didn't know anything about it. But still my name got pulled into the conversation because three days ago, I witnessed the same Candice arguing with someone else in the room. After my roomie returned from dining, all of them were talking and working on arts and craft – She may or may not have been watching TV but, it was Candice's T.V. day and one of my students ran into the room and said "The movie Exodus is on television." We'd been talking about this in class today and will be discussing it for the rest of our lesson for tomorrow. She was so excited.

When a commercial came on, I turned the channel to look for the movie Exodus. Remember, everyone was working on art, not watching the TV at all (ok, maybe they were listening to it, but a commercial was on). As soon as I turned the channel, all hell broke loose out of Candice. I only turned the TV while a commercial was on the channel just to see what my students were saying. I wanted to find out when it would come back on. I then flipped back and saw where it was still on a commercial. Candice proceeded to go off with her mouth. I wanted to get in my flesh and knock her teeth out. But thank God, I'm conscious about the future with tonight service and class again tomorrow. It just would not look good for the preacher to go to lock down for beating up this mouthy child. She is so childlike and I feel sorry for her. But I'm going to ask God to help me to prevail to be the bigger person. Actually, (In retrospect, I should have asked since it was her TV day). I'm doing my best to keep theses ear buds in my ear and just stay clear of all drama and conversations especially while I'm fasting. The devil is on the attack and I know that! I'm doing my best to keep this flesh under subjection. Jesus take the wheel. I'm getting under my covers to rest and sleep until church time about one hour from now. This is another way of fighting, without fighting.

March 5, 2017 – I'm blessed of the Lord and highly favored. I just love Jesus so much. Oh my God. What a wonderful savior. I don't do TV much. (Compared to those who practically lived in front of it). Sundays are the only time I really desire to watch anything on TV. I enjoy watching Dr. Tony Evans, the Urban Alternative Ministry. He always speaks into my life. The last time he spoke about Joseph which was the very situation that I equate my life to today. This session ran the first Sunday in March. Today, he's talking about an "Eternal Perspective." A view of your future will change and transform your present. He called the lesson, "Motivation for Ministry." I called it getting ready for heaven. The text was **Colossian 1:24-29.** The goal of this text was to **"present every man complete when we all stand at judgement."** Will you be a spiritual success or a spiritual failure?

If the enemy can get you to not look at a future then your today will look like whatever. If you have no goal, no target, you'll hit it every time because you are shooting at nothing. *If you forget to acknowledge there is a tomorrow, you will live anyway you want today.*

What a wonderful surprise! Paula Cook showed up about 11:30 a.m. today. I wasn't expecting a visit. I'm so glad to see her. It's been great. I was fasting and maybe should have continued the fast but being in a position to eat "free world food" was upon me. I had a pizza and a corn dog, chips, candy and a soda. Except for the Pizza and Corn dog, I could have ordered all this on the store tomorrow, forgive me Lord, for breaking this weekend fast. I do understand the purpose of fasting and prayer. I know it's killing my flesh. Fasting doesn't move God at all, his providential ruling will prevail. However, fasting does position me to keep my mouth/flesh under subjection. Keep me humble and keep me in the word even more than usual because the word is my food all day long. So, even though I've eaten, I'm still committed to getting into His presence, reading and living his word, Amen. It's 6:00 p.m. now and I'm about to go to church service.

March 6, 2017 be unreasonably committed – Proverbs 4:7-9. This has been a great day. I've been sleepy all day. At 2:00 p.m., I washed, blow dried my hair and paid $2.00 for a stylist to flat iron my hair beautifully. I ate dinner early at 5:00 p.m. I attended the "Women's Empowerment" class. At 6:30 p.m., I attended

"Intercessory prayer." At 7:00 p.m., I attended rehearsal for the Black History program with Ms. Hill until 8:00 p.m. Before I could get out the gym, the "Jericho Walk" group came in and we prayed, walked our laps and then went to the day room to heat my coffee. Before I knew it, it's count time again at 9:00 p.m. While I want to write letters tonight, I'm so sleepy. I'll go to bed and call it a night after count. Maybe I can get up early and restart.

March 7, 2017 – "Bless the Lord oh my soul and all that is within me, bless the Lord oh my soul and forget not all of his benefits. This is the day that the Lord had made. I will rejoice and be glad in it."

6:30 a.m. – I showered, groomed and awaited the call to breakfast. While I waited, I chose to eat my "spiritual breakfast" now. 8:00 a.m., count time. 9:00 to 10:00 a.m., I had my "Wellness walk." My shoulder and across the top of my back hurts and I don't know why; that's a first. I wonder if all that aerobic exercise is catching up with me. Its 11:00 a.m.

I've slept for 30 minutes. I had to be awakened for 11:30 a.m. count. Wow, I'm exhausted. I've also heard that Ms. Giles left, as expected, going to court and will be back as she anticipates, I hope. Before she left, she'd already given me the folder for the Black History program and attendance sheet for the choir as well. I expect adversity, but I'm already prayed up. Scrabble was fun. I won. Now, I'm waiting for 3:00 p.m. count, dinner and then rehearsal for choir. We're practicing for the Black History program in March.

By the majority of my peers, I was selected to serve as the Mistress of Ceremony.

March 11, 2017 – 8:00 a.m. – Wednesday, Thursday and Friday, March 8-10, 2017, I didn't pull out my journal at all. It was routine except for the practice for the Black History Program we had on yesterday, Friday, March 10. I was busy from the time I woke up until I went to bed. I showered, groomed, dressed, made my bed and ate breakfast. I had a medical checkup because my right ear has been "clogged" since I washed my hair on Monday. Nurse Nelms said my ears were as clear as a bell, better than any inmates she'd ever seen. No wax build-up, so clear she could see my ear drum with the otoscope.

There was no buildup at all so she guessed it was sinus draining. I told her, I have no history of having sinus trouble. My nose is clear not stuffed. It's a mystery to me. I sound so hollow like I'm speaking in a vacuum. It's really difficult to hear myself even sing. Now we have this Black History Program/Martin Luther King Program and it's going to be a blast. Comedy, skits, singing and dancing of course with some serious speeches of some ladies telling their own history which made this program one of the best years according to a lot of the staff and the inmates. God blessed us and I believe he was glorified.

Ms. Hill gave the participants, hot popcorn afterwards. Now 10:30 a.m. and time to prepare for 11:00 a.m. count time. I just replied to Sharon Beaner's e-mail.

I completed my message I'm preaching tonight and now I'm going to finish some letters. I've started writing Dr. Lynn, Angela, Ann and Jimmy Wilson, two of my most precious clients. Hopefully, I'll get them all done and mailed out next week. The most intimidating letter I have been waiting to write is to Bishop Bronner. I so want to write him. I'm just not sure where to begin.

Father God, help me to say what I need to say and when. Class today was all feedback from students, it was great.

March 12, 2017 – Routine, detail, visitation set up. I read and rested. I watched Dr. Tony Evans as usual every Sunday a.m. 7:30 to 8:30 a.m. He is consistent with his ministry. I love it! God is so faithful. My desire is his desire. I will trust you Lord in every area of my life!

March 13, 2017 - I'm resting, reading and have had very little contact with anybody. I slept and chilled out until class time when we had the "Women of Empowerment" class. I then worked on my Vision board. Then back to my bunk with limited connection with anyone today.

March 14, 2017 – I had breakfast and went back to bed. I had no outside walking today. I'm working on my Vision board and a paper about myself. No lunch and no drama. I'm just focused on getting it done beautifully and effectively honest so I can really use this Vision Board when I'm out of here. I believe God is going to move on my release very soon.

March 15, 2017 – It's been a roller coaster of a day, while I've listened to Jekalyn Carr all day. ***They said, but God said*** is the song that brought me to tears.

The thing I had to remember is that God is in control and there is no way he is going to let his word fall to the ground.

I tried to reach Jekalyn Carr to request permission to use the lyric to her song in this book. Unfortunately, the numbers I've called and the email I've sent has not responded in writing, nevertheless, if you really want to be blessed beyond measure purchase her music and listen to the words of this song. I still listen to this song often, it speaks to what I've gone through and will still no doubt have a great impact on the days, months, and years to come because it speaks truth.

It's life; we are all going to face hurt, pain, heartaches and rain. Life is full of ups and downs, friends here today but tomorrow they may not be found. I'm sure you can relate to have cried tears where you've been wronged and when you thought someone would be there for you and you ended up walking alone, but just know that GOD is still GOD and he will never leave nor forsake you.

When it feels like you want to throw in the towel, remember this season is just for a while. All of us have seasons and just because you're a Christian, don't think it's going to be a cake walk. Just when you think it's not in you, that's the time God will raise you up for his glory. People may count you out, but know that God has purpose for your life. (I can prophecy to myself)

Anyway, after listening to Jekalyn Carr song over and over and over again, I cried almost a half a roll of toilet paper. Then, after talking to Dedric last night, he told me how he went to the Parole Board today to discuss my case. They told him "they no longer meet with families." I cried again and again.

I was so sad which is why I think I was crying all day long. I knew I had the Warden's "Woman of Empowerment" class and will speak to the Warden or Deputy Warden today to find out my status about TPM, release day or whatever. I had been saying how I trust God, now here is where testing will tell if I am trusting God or not.

I presented my Vision board to the class, crying uncontrollably I might add. I didn't know why I just broke down like a dam. Well, after the class, Deputy

Warden Hendrix called me into her office and told me how I was the only one in our "Women Empowerment" class of twelve who currently qualified for any movement.

I was told, "with your six pic-points applied, (pic= parole incentive credit), each credit is worth one month off, this will take six months off the sentence". So, the remaining 24 months is now equal to 18 months left. To qualify as a candidate to even have the privilege to be transferred to a transitional center, I'm told you can only have a maximum of 18 months left on your sentence. Deputy Hendrix signed me up right away on her desk computer and turned the screen for me to see. "There; it's done" but she told me, "Don't tell anyone." Once I cried, I said okay and left her office.

Thank you, Jesus. I'm so happy. Movement only happened on Tuesday or Thursday, I could be out of here as early as tomorrow, I thought to myself.

March 16, 2017 – After watching Greenleaf last night, I took a late 11:00 p.m. shower, climbed into my bunk and slept like a baby. The peace of knowing I'm leaving here very soon was wonderful.

I got up for breakfast, located music on the kiosk, Oleta Adams singing, "Holy is the Lamb" and Yolanda Adams singing "Be Still."

I went back to the dorm to get ready for inspection. I've packed up my locker. I had things for Ozzie to take home Sunday. My knee had become more painful and impossible to get down on my knees to pray. I can't take Aerobic exercise anymore. I limit my walking until I can see the doctor next week.

The pain woke me up out of my sleep a few nights ago. Prayerfully, the doctor will give me an anti-inflammatory that will make my knee feel better. OK, let me finish my letters and get them in the mail Friday morning.

March 17, 2017 – I showered early, groomed, dressed, ate breakfast and just sat around to rest. My right knee was still in pain. My acquaintance, Lakeekee Steward, has some pain pills/Anti-Inflammatory Naprosyn 375 mg. My 250 mg are gone and didn't work at all. I hope these higher milligrams will help. I am going to just eat, sleep and rest today.

Popcorn – Yeah! A whole big bag of it, thanks Stacy Utley. She's a lifer, she served 22 years already and who knows how many more. I'm going to keep in touch with her when I leave. I pray she will one day actually be released; only God knows.

March 20, 2017 – Happy 5th Wedding Anniversary Edith and Ozzie. Saturday was full from sun up to sun down, but I'm having an amazing day. After breakfast and setting up visitation and detail, I returned back to my dorm and prepared for a Kairos Reunion. I was given my message just this am. It was a fresh message from God, "Patience." Then God reminded me of a song sister Laketa Leslie wrote and gave me in 2013 called "It's not in Vain." The song and the message were well received. So many women here have hidden treasures. Megan F. spoke about her painful history, but she has emerged so victoriously. She is a determined an empowered woman, who needs to go on Dr. Phil TV show to help so many others. Lisa R. has written amazing poetry that needs to be published. We had such an awesome day. The Lord has spoken though so many overcoming women.

This weekend Saturday and Sunday was full. Sunday was an amazing day. Sunday was my first time seeing my husband and sister, Gwen in a year. We hugged and I didn't cry as I imagined I would. We took pictures, had limited conversation and time seem to drag until 3:00 p.m., when they left.

This is the last day of my teaching the weekend class. The students had everything prepared. A party was set up so beautifully, it was fit for a queen. The students had written on the board, Ms. Ohio, (I'm originally from Toledo OH), greatest facilitator ever, super teacher, and other accolades had been written with the names of the graduates on the board. Music was playing. I could not have done the set up any better. I'm so pleased. Three attendees talked to the class. We collected final papers and enjoyed an awesome celebration. Then graduation began. After graduation, we began to talk of the greatness of the class material and how much they've all learned. I will not take God's Glory. I even read a piece of my journal, admitting to an adversity I've overcome. It was a powerful closing. I asked each student to "pick one student and tell them what they admired and what growth you saw in them, through this class." I also wanted to know "what could be improved about the class. Oh, my God. What a reception! Power poured into this room. God moved so powerfully.

Leaders were developed. These are the future speakers loud and clear. "OVERCOMING ADVERSITIES" MINISTRIES...JESUS TAKE THE WHEEL!

Well, it's now Monday morning 7:00 a.m. – I think it's the last class for Radicals. Since Brunette left, Giles took over the class and then Giles left to go to court. So, there was no class. Jennifer, I heard was supposed to take over for Giles, but had to go to G.E.D. class. For whatever reason, suddenly the prison was put on lockdown. Therefore, there was no movement. No one went anywhere during lockdown. It was rumored that some gang activity was going on in the male prison and I'm told when that happens, security guards are "compromised" and since there's already not enough staff, movement has to be limited.

Therefore, it is the last of all the classes this week. Who knows, I hope it's my last week here at E.M.F. I just believe I'm going to be taken this week. **To God be the glory for this thing he has done.** Hallelujah!!

I'm so looking forward to leaving E.W.F. Tonight would not be too soon! I've completed and closed "Overcoming Adversities" class which I facilitated. I've packaged the class material and feedback to give to Ms. Wadley, my counselor to pass on to the next facilitator.

If I don't get an opportunity to speak to her, I've written my notes of closure and have said my good-byes to those I've grown fond of. I've collected my books and I'm prepared to pack out with the food I have. I'd almost like one more week to order another $60 store. I got the chance to speak to my sister Cynthia and my friends Brunette and Eterica at the Atlanta T.C. Transitional center through Cynthia's three-way phone. They told me the food at the T.C. is horrible and I need to bring as much as possible. So, either way, I'm ok. The GED graduation is Friday where the choir sings and then Saturday is Joy night. So, if I don't leave tonight, that's okay. I'm still one more step closer to home, knowing it won't be long. All is well. No problem either way. God knows what's best!

March 21, 2017 – Well, I'm still here, but there's still one more opportunity to go this week on Thursday. If not, then I'll definitely be here for the Joyous weekend and another store order. OK, let's not put the cart before the horse. I don't want to get ahead of God. Breakfast right now is oatmeal with another dry cake, half an orange and a flat sausage patty. I think I'll pass. I have my own donuts and coffee in my locker. Better yet, I'll eat spiritually and fill up on the word and some worship music.

This was the first day I've returned to walk this year. My right knee has been diagnosed with tendonitis and it's giving out lots of pain when I try to bend/jump on it. So, I'll just walk and stop Aerobics for good. I can't wait to go swimming again. This is the best exercise for me with this condition.

The doctor looked at this knee again today and ordered an MRI to look at the cartilage and tendons. He prescribed Meloxicam, an anti-inflammatory. My Blood Pressure is still a little high 166/88. I'm hoping I get my meds, store and have a blessed weekend with the graduation, our inmate service and then leave here on Tuesday morning. I was once told "if you want to make God laugh, tell him your plans." Oh well, choir rehearsal and Scrabble with Sheree. Now it's time for bed – Good night.

March 22, 2017 – It's a cereal breakfast, potatoes, sausage, grits and hot coffee. My room is inspection ready. It's nice enough to get dorm of the week. I'm listening to music meditating in God's presence. It's a quiet and uneventful day. The Warden's "Women Empowerment" class was called to come to listen to Lakeisha presentation. (Lakeisha was hospitalized with kidney stones during the time of the class's presentation). She would show her Vision Board and present.

Then it was time for Choir rehearsal and next we had Kairos. Once it was 8:00 p.m., we have count and then I cleaned my area and got ready for bed. I was exhausted and went to my bunk to rest. But, it's 9:00 p.m. and Empire is back on. 10:00 p.m., Greenleaf is on also. So, now it's 11:00 p.m. and I'm definitely ready to sleep. Good night.

March 23, 2017 – Breakfast was not great. Biscuit and grape jelly, grits and coffee. Rooms and the locker were inspected and I'm going out for the Wellness walk. It's cold outside and my right knee is feeling discomfort. I'm going back inside. Once inside, I spotted the whole major inspection team. So, as they went into H-dorm, I went to the library and remained there reading until an officer came to take a group out and back to the dorm. I'm sleepy. I'm listening to my word on my player while I journaled.

March 24, 2017 – It's graduation day for ten offenders getting their GED. Actually one, Renee, (a black girl), is graduating from the Georgia Veteran program. She is receiving a Master's in Public Health. She is also a grant writer. She told a little of her history. She told me what brought her to prison.

She said, "In the heat of anger, she got caught up in a fight that took a turn for the worse with a knife and she's here on aggravated assault." She is 30 months in on a 36-month sentence. What a shame. Another white female is here for manslaughter on a five - month old infant, but is doing less time. What a disparity amongst race. It's so unfair. I'm convinced there is no justice to an "unjust system." How do we fight injustice?

Lord, what needs to be done to stop this! God says, they did it to my son too. They meaning the world didn't want to hear the truth. If they hated him, they are going to hate you also. Don't get distracted, stay close in my word. Hear my voice and follow me. **"I will teach thee, I will lead thee, I will guide thee with mine eyes said the Lord!"**

I know Jesus is soon to return and **"the harvest is so plentiful, "but the laborers are few."** Am I really to go to Law School or am I to only study God's law? Lord, please make it plain to me. I know what God said, 30 years ago (Study Joshua 1:8) and I know what I saw inside here during this incarceration. Lord, give me clarity on the Law you are speaking about today....

March 25, 2017 – Another day the Lord has made. "I will rejoice and be glad in it." I do not know why I was sad yesterday. I just had a moment of sadness where I just wanted to cry. My right knee was aggravated. But that was only a pinch of the issue. I didn't want to call my baby sister or anybody else for that matter.

Just a spirit of "sadness." Later that day, Stacy Utley gave me two big bags of popcorn and not even that "lifted my spirit." I went to bed and just wept before the Lord. I slept and meditated on the word of God. I got up and went to dinner, sat down to eat, but had no appetite. I gave away all my food and left the chow hall. I retired to bed. Today, I'm spending time in the word of God. Even to those who don't want to hear it as God directs. Reading my word, listening to Joel Osteen, I will just wait in God's divine presence until he speaks something more to me.   Joy night was awesome tonight, oh my goodness. Not a dry eye in the house, and the multi-purpose room was full, God moved in these ladies.

March 27, 2017 – Tuesday morning and I'm still here. Boy, I really thought I'd be gone to the T.C. by this morning. I even told my sister and my son, "I'm out of here!" Ok Lord, I get it. Not until you say so. I'm good. I'll yet praise you and give you the glory.

March 29, 2017 – People are waking up in an ugly mood today. I packed last night thinking I was going to T.C. for sure. I sent out final e-mails. I got all my "goodbyes" out of the way and its 4:30 a.m. and still no tap on the shoulder to go. Oh wow, I'm going to quit expecting that tap on the shoulder early in the morning. I am putting all my stuff back into the back of the locker and getting my bible out to read. There's something God still has for me to do here. Ok, speak God. I'm going to just wait, pray and seek God. Not another day will I speak about leaving. Just wait until it happens. I will absolutely worship while I wait.

March 31, 2017 – Today we received our food packages. Everyone is like a kid on Christmas morning when these packages arrive. (I'm waiting to be called for my pick-up). Once back in the dorm with our packages, people began trading and eating all day. I'm packing 98 percent of my stuff to go with me to the T.C. I'm sharing very little - sorry. I'm always giving. Today, I'm going to keep my stuff for me.

CHAPTER 7
SHAKE IT OFF!

April 1, 2017 – Another month gone and a new month here today. I showered, shampooed, blow dried and curled my hair then back to bed I went. I decided to sleep in, resting, reading and getting ready to preach tonight. Lord, what is it that you would have me to say to your people tonight? I was quiet, only listening to the word of God on my player, reading the scripture and napping in between – nothing yet. I'm not "cooking" anything today. I'm only eating my popcorn my friend Tracy gave me. I'm also snacking off the food package I received yesterday.

I feel like writing to Bishop Bronner. I think I'll start my letter tomorrow. I'm praying and seeking God. It's not about my preaching tonight, it's about getting into his presence and hearing from the Lord. It's not about what I have to say. I'd rather hear what the word wants to say. I want God to speak to our hearts. God, let us just worship you is my prayer.

We had 15 minutes of straight praise and worship lifting our hands, voices, and giving him all the glory, honor and praise. Lord, you have your way all day!

Tonight, I spoke with Cynthia and Dedric. They are still my main team. Thank you, Jesus. I spoke to mom and Gwen earlier today they are fine. I'm happy to say, this has been the first day of a new month and all is well. I'm so excited to be going to the T.C. this week, I hope.

April 2, 2017 – I wanted no breakfast again this morning. I slept in and it was great. I watched Dr. Tony Evans at 7:30 a.m., I studied my word, worshipped and then went back to sleep. After 11:00 a.m. we had count. I then showered and curled my hair. Maybe, just maybe, I'll get a surprise visit. I'm making tuna for lunch, with chips. Minister Tammy McMillan fixed fried rice she wanted us to eat together. So, we shared an enjoyable lunch. After lunch I was resting, watched a little TV and tried to call mom, Gwen, and Ozzie. Still, no one is answering at 5:30 p.m.

Maybe they are at a Sunday service together. I'm going to listen to my word on the tablet until 7:00 p.m. church time tonight.

Free Indeed church came and ministered the last Seven Words of Jesus with scripture reference and it was over. I spent a quiet evening reading and studying with a snack. I decided to turn in early.

April 3, 2017 – "This is the day the Lord has made and I will rejoice and be glad in it." I want nothing for breakfast. They are serving oatmeal and Bran Flakes.

When my bunkie came back, she said it was grits and eggs. It was my fault; I didn't go to see for myself, so I missed that. I ate peanut butter cracker with cheese and hot coffee. I feel inspired to write to Bishop Bronner today. I pray he receives it and responds. This is going to be a cereal day and I pray it will be my last night sleeping here. It's my prayer that I wake up at three o'clock a.m. to be told to pack it up. It's time to go. Stored just delivered, yeah!

April 4, 2017 – Another day the Lord has made, I will rejoice and be glad in it. The devil is starting early this morning. I'm usually up and in the shower at 4:30 a.m. But today, I slept in and decided to take a bird bath. I'm in the bathroom for eleven minutes and someone is knocking at the door which irritated me. This is why I'm usually in the shower at 4:30 a.m. Once I came out, someone made a mean comment about the length of time I was in the bath room. I responded to the comment and went straight off especially when someone remarked sarcastically, "You're supposed to be a Godly woman." Of course, I defended myself. "I am a Godly woman but, I'm no rug. You're not going to walk on me. If you don't want to wait, then get your butts up at 5:00 a.m. when the lights come on at 5:00 wakeup call. Otherwise, don't say anything to me about taking 11 minutes in the bathroom." My bunkie added her two cents and said, "13 minutes." "Oh, ok, I responded. So, I was two minutes longer than I stated." I said again, "get your butts up early like I usually do. Otherwise, wait and don't say anything else to me," with the facial expression to match my words. Of course, others chimed in to say that "it's not all about you today." Arguing ensued; I was escalating, probably because I thought I was going to the T.C. last night.

Well, there is still one more opportunity to leave on Thursday morning. Movement to the T.C. only happened on Tuesdays and Thursdays. Everything that's over my head is under Christ's foot, that's why he walked on the water. It's not even seven a.m. and this page is almost full. What a way to start the day.

Breakfast was horrible. They served grits that was not seasoned. The biscuit was thick and not done. The coffee did not have any sugar. I feel like I should have stayed in bed. I'm just waiting now for 8:00 a.m. count. I am currently listening to my theme song, "Trust in You" by Lauren Daigle.

No detail today, no appointments, no classes, nothing today on my schedule. Oh, Lord, I'll spend time with you today. Spending quality time listening to your voice is my desire to you Lord. I hear my name called over the intercom. "Edith Page, report to the multipurpose room." When I get there, I am asked to set up for visitation, my former detail, so they can take pictures.

No problem, done. Back to the dorm and wrote my letters and waited for lunch. Turkey wraps, potato salad and carrots were served. Lunch was decent today.

April 5, 2017 – Another day the Lord has made. "I will rejoice and be glad in it." In spite of how my flesh feels, my spirit will rejoice because I command it to! This body has to obey what I say, not how I feel. I've completed a five-page letter to Bishop Bronner finally. I will mail it off tomorrow morning. After attempting to write it at three, six and nine months, finally it's the twelfth month, it's done. I'm going to pray he receives it and responds accordingly.

God inspired me to go outside. I walked two miles, after I'd stop going out a few weeks ago. I've been "in the dumps" about still being here. I think I got ahead of myself. After being told on March 15 that I was approved to go to the TC, (three weeks ago today), I'm still here. So, I'm back to my song "I will Trust in you" by Lauren Daigle." God may be sparing me from something down the road that I can't see or maybe there's more to my assignment that I need to complete here. Whatever it is, yes Lord, Yes and Amen. I'm done worrying about it. I am going to relax with worship music in my ears, Lord. Have your way, I'm plugging out everybody and listening keenly for your voice.

April 6, 2017 – When I woke up at 5:15 a.m., I rushed to the shower, groomed and dressed by 5:40 a.m. I read my bible while listening to the bible on my tablet until time to go outside and walk for wellness. I walked four miles today. I've decided to go back to all that I was doing before I was told I'm all signed up to go to the T.C. I sung in the choir, re-joined the prayer team, had classes and other activities. Maybe once I take my mind off of it, then that's when it will happen. When God is ready for me to go, that's when it will happen not a moment sooner. I just will continue in prayer and patience.

*One of my favorite scriptural prayer **I Kings 8:23 "Lord, God of Israel, there is no God like thee, in heaven above, or on the earth beneath who keepest covenant and mercy with thy servants who walk before thee with all their heart."***

It is 5:15 a.m. - After getting up, I showered and dressed for the day. This is what the Lord dropped in my spirit.

Amos 8: Verse 11, says; ... I will send a famine in the land, not a famine of bread, nor a thirst for water, but of hearing the words of the Lord. I can tell you assuredly, that this shall come to pass; God will do everything that His word says he will do. No matter how people continue to rebel, not believe, and live as if He's not coming back. Every word of God shall come to pass.

Friday, April 7, 2018 – I woke up very early this morning at 3:15 a.m. I laid up looking to see what God wants to say. I listened to the book of Acts on my player. **"If this be of man, it will surely come to naught; but if it be of God, nobody can over throw it and you'll be fighting against God."**

Father, I rejoice that you have counted me worthy to suffer for your glory. While I don't think more highly of myself than I ought, I'm not "too good" to clean and serve. But I do know I'm a servant of God and must do as the Lord commands, not man.

During my specific bible study time, all my roomies know not to disturb me. Someone said something indirectly about me getting up to help clean. I didn't even reply, but here's what I read next.

Act 6:2 - It is not reason that I should leave the word of God and serve tables. Verse 4. But I will give myself continually to pray and to the ministry of the word. I love it when the Lord fights for me. I'm learning every day that the battle is not mine. *I don't have to open my mouth at all.* For those who try to attack my character, my integrity and my personality, they lose. It doesn't matter because the word proves me to be correct every time. They don't realize they are only hurting themselves, the bible says. It's better that they put a millstone about their own neck, cast themselves into the depth of the sea, than to put their mouth on me. Just give time, time and time will tell it all.

It's not yet 6:00 a.m. and I've been up and flowing for a few hours. What does God have in store for me today? It's been quiet in my spirit resting in my bunk reading, meditating, saying very little to anyone.

Only answering questions with one or two words as necessary to respond. If I can say nothing, I say absolutely nothing. The less said the better.

Lord, you are so faithful and you will keep me covered by your blood and covered in the word of God. Father, I thank you God things are as well as they are. I will not complain.

I heard over the intercom "Women of Empowerment," report to the multi -purpose room. We are being fed by the Warden for our graduating class on March 15, 2017. That was also the date I was told I'm going to the T.C. (I couldn't eat the shredded BBQ pork with Sweet Baby Rays sauce I had previously prepared) because we had a big Chik' Fil-a sandwich, hug chocolate chip cookie with chips and lemonade. Another occasion where outside food was brought in. We have a new young warden who is so good to all the inmates. This food was so good and I'm stuffed. Wow, how great is my God. I'm so full.

Later at 7:00 p.m., I'm not hungry. I'm resting, eating popcorn and reading. I don't have to be hungry to eat popcorn; it's just such an enjoyable treat anytime.

April 8, 2017 – Another day in this place. God, you're still good to me. I rested, read, relaxed, spoke to mom, Gwen, Cynthia and Ozzie. I ate my own food from yesterday, BBQ pork, and Idaho four cheese mashed potatoes and shared half with Tracey Utley. Nothing more was needed, just resting, reading my book until time to get ready for church. Shavonne Giles taught, "Can You Handle the Truth of God Word."? Tammy spoke, "Maintain the Change." Then we had praise and worship. It was all good, I ate a snack and I'm ready for bed.

April 9, 2017 – I'm excited! Paula is coming to visit today. Breakfast was good. I ate it all. I came back and watched Dr. Tony Evans. "Live Earthly with a Heavenly Perspective." He's always been a great teacher. I've always walked away from the end of his program refreshed, renewed and revived. My prospective has had a heavenly view, a special reverence of God which is why I've been married four times. I literally believe God's word. **I Corinthians 6:18 says Flee fornication. Every sin a man doeth is without the body; but he that committeth fornication sinneth against his own body.** This is why I've been married almost as many times as

Elizabeth Taylor. I've been afraid to fornicate. My body and spirit belong to God.

Anyway, I'm thankful to God that he has me in his care and all is well. My tablet player is on again. Yes, this is my passion listening to the word in my ears.

Paula has arrived! I was caught up in the Shekinah Glory of Jesus when the officer tapped me on my knee and said to go to visitation. Thank God for Paula Cook!

After an awesome spirit filled visionary visit, I cooked for five people and we feasted naturally and spiritually. You can probably tell by now that food is a real big deal here in prison. Food in here is like "freedom" out there.

April 10, 2017 – Its 5:00 a.m. I have showered, groomed, and I have dressed already so I'll listen to Shekinah Glory again this a.m. on my fully charged tablet that's working again by the anointing of the Holy Ghost. Oh, did I not tell you what happened with my tablet? A few days ago, it was acting up. I could not get it to stay on. It was fully charged or it appeared to be, with a full green bar. But I couldn't get it to come on. It appeared to come on, light up for a few seconds and then goes off. The screen was completely black, no action at all. Then I prayed on it. I reminded God that I'd just purchased an album for $12.30, Shekinah Glory. I needed my worship music to listen to my bible on my tablet as I read along with it. I asked several people to help to no avail. In fact, Barbara said, "this tablet is dead." I immediately nullified those words and said "no honey, my table shall live and not die." Within a few minutes, I got it to come on and it stayed on. I quickly downloaded the album and breakfast was called.   I completed the download, went to my dorm and tossed the player on my bunk and went to breakfast. Once I returned, I could not get the device to turn back on. I tried all day, to no avail. The player would not turn on. I used someone else charger. I checked everything that could be wrong with it.   But still, the tablet *appeared* to be dead.

I heard people say how these refurbished tablets were no good. Different inmates began to say how it was dead and I needed to put in a trouble ticket in to Jay pay to get another one. I'd already done that once in February when they replied "it's no longer under warranty and I'd have to purchase a new one." Then a day later, someone told me of a Veteran, who has a new player never synced before and wanted to sale it for $90.00. I was all for getting a new tablet but wasn't willing to give up mine with all my data and songs on it. I made the attempt to buy it, went to the Kiosk with her, but God stopped that. I thought now, God, I've known you by the testimony of others to raise up dead cars, dead wash machines, and you are the creator of all things, you can restore my tablet.   Guess what happened, I laid hands on this tablet, several times and commanded it to work. Glory be to God. It's working and I'm telling everybody who will listen.

God did it! Hallelujah. The blood still works! The power of God is all that and a bag of chips! It's time to go to dinner this evening. Praise the Lord!

April 11, 2017 - Another day that the Lord has made, "**I will rejoice and be glad in it.**" God is still good. I woke up at 4:55 a.m. I again was hoping to be awakened in the wee hours to pack it up for T.C. Nevertheless, I'm still here and I'm going to make the best of it. Somehow, I forgot about the "Warden's Newsletter" class and "Intercessory prayer." I didn't even go outside yesterday. I just enjoyed being in the presence of the Lord.

Today, I walked briskly at 9:00 a.m. and 2:00 p.m. yard call. I got five miles in today. I went out for all three meals. (Yesterday, I missed dinner.) I am on my way to choir rehearsal and I'm going to have a simple light weight snack. Then I will just lay down with my book. I probably need to call family since I've not spoken to them since Friday.

Paula's visit on Sunday actually helped set the week off right. This pen I'm writing with now is nice and was "sold" to me by Michelle for a package of tuna. I hope it's not taken away in a shake down as I don't know where she got it from. Family Day is April 21.

I didn't have my family RSVP because I thought I'd already be gone. I pray I'm not here in two more weeks. Jesus take the wheel! Goodnight.

April 12, 2017 – Exactly one year ago, I was taken into custody from the courtroom in Marietta, to Cobb County Jail. Twenty-three days later, I was transferred to Lee Arrendale State Prison. May 5, 2016, I had to be stripped naked, coughed, squat, spread my cheeks and lips of your most private area, lifted my breast, deloused and dressed in clothing called a prison uniform.
Attorney's said, "You'll only be there a short time." But it feels like a "lifetime."

*I can let my mind wonder or I can bring every thought captive to the obedience of the word of God. **Die** is the center world of obe**die**nce. My flesh is now dead to the why and how much longer. I will not let my flesh rule and get me all upset about still being here. Lord is there more that you require of me? Then, I'm willing and obedient. I trust you to do whatever it is that you have purposed for my life. **Now Devil, take that!** I've let go of my own desire, dreams and destiny and I'm saying yes Lord to whatever and however you have planned and purposed for me. If the Lord will... then this or that. "My life is not my own. To you Lord I belong, I give myself away so you can use me." Last night I received mail from two of my family members. I received an Easter Card from my blessed sister in the Lord, Ressie*

Clement and energizing heart felt words of love from Crystal Smith, a super friend from Toledo, Ohio. God is in control and all is well!

It's 4:15 a.m. - I'm showered, groomed dressed and journaled. Now, I'm ready to rest in his presence. To God be the Glory! **This is the day that the Lord has made, I will rejoice and be glad in it.** Breakfast was good this morning. The diced potatoes were golden brown. I ate mine and someone else's too. The grits were not as well cooked as usual, but eatable. I cut up the sausage and placed them in my grits and had coffee. I need to get my locker inspection ready. Now I'm going out for my wellness walk. Unfortunately, my locker is so stocked, I refused to open it. The inspection team came so quick today; I didn't have time to cover anything even if I wanted to. I stood at attention and made no eye contact. It worked. They walked through and focused on another inmate's locker and the bathroom floor. The Warden could spot a single hair in a bathroom. They didn't say anything to me. Yeah! Nevertheless, I will plan to get my locker inspection ready at some point today. Wellness walk, finally called. I was able to get in ten laps and later in the afternoon eight more laps. I am not sure if it makes a difference since I've eaten double meals at dinner. I did enjoy "Intercessory pray" and church service with the Akins tonight. It's now 9:00 p.m., count time and no TV, no Empire until p.m. count is clear. Guess I'll just enjoy Greenleaf at 10:00 p.m. and then go to bed. Lord if it's my night for T.C., thank you. If not, hallelujah anyhow.

April 13, 2017 – Another day's journey and I'm glad about it. **"This is the day the Lord has made, I will rejoice and be glad in it."** This is another opportunity to put the devil under my foot. Since I wasn't tapped on the shoulder and awakened to leave for the T.C., I'm done thinking and talking about it. Now, if I'm still here April 21 on family day, I'd like my husband to be able to come. Deputy Warden Hendrix told me to ask Counselor Wadley and she'd probably let him come. Well, it's now 4:55 p.m. and I think she leaves at 5:00 p.m. So, I'll write a note and slip it under her door. If I put it in the box, she may or may not get if before her deadline to turn in for count of heads on tomorrow. The "run around," the (A - F dorm), as it is fondly called are having their family day tomorrow and the choir is singing. Since I'm in the choir, maybe we will be allowed to stay and look, listen, and eat to. It's been a good day.

It's my TV day and I'm in control of the remote.   It was nice to not watch any Prison TV, Hip Hop and Drama TV shows that my roomies are always watching. These girls are in prison. Why do they want to watch all this crazy prison and Lifetime crime dramas?   Steve Harvey is my favorite.

Yes, I watched "Black" TV, the Bounce station Vivica Fox – "Two Can Play that Game" with Morris Chestnut and double-take with Eddie Griffin. Then it was time for choir rehearsal. Later, we watched one episode of Family Feud and again at 8:00 p.m. A few inmates wanted to watch 60 Days in. I hate that show. Of course, I said NO! Greys Anatomy was one that was a winner and Scandal is scandalous. Olivia Pope is pretty as she can be. However, the whole show is all about dirt, lies, murder, adultery, homosexuality, and I said to my roommates, nobody needs to watch all that mess. They did switch between the two channels until I fell asleep.

April 14, 2017 – I'm in no hurry to get up today but my routine still dictates a 4:30 a.m. shower, make my bed, etc. Folks in my room are starting their lunches as early as 9:45 a.m. I'm not eating just to be eating. I'll wait until noon or so. Jessica is waiting for Michelle and Jennie LeAnn Hooper. Jessica's girlfriend is a little "salty" this morning. Since it's just the two of them, I may eat with them. They are having a chicken bowl with rice.

Well, the choir is now being paged to report out to the gym to sing for Family day for the run-around. Next Friday is April 21st. It's the H-dorm's turn for the Family festival. I hope I'm gone by then. If not, I hope Ozzie can come. Cynthia and Dedric will not be in Georgia.

Well, the choir is allowed to stay in the Gym for Family day after singing. However, I was very disappointed in the food. Cheap and half cooked hot dogs, the cheapest cookies and drink aid on the market. No quality about anything, that's un-usual. The graduation receptions or even the Family day of last year was much better. After it was over, we had to go through "shakedown" before we could leave the gym area. Shakedown was just what it sounds like, stripped naked and violated looking for contraband that families may have slipped in coming for family day. That was an ordeal. Yes, it's happened before. I don't plan to do that again. In fact, I'm going to absolutely cancel any and everybody's visitation from this day on. I will see you on the other side. I hate being strip searched.

April 15, 2017 – Another day the Lord has made one more chance and another opportunity to get it right.

By now, I guess you can tell I am feeling a little low. Lord, please hear my prayer:

Father, in the name of Jesus, I start this day with you first, seeking your face and not your hand, Lord. I need you to speak to my heart, mind, soul and spirit. My desire is one with your desire no matter what this flesh tries to rise up and say. My heart's desire is to do my purpose that you created me to do.

*I humble myself to the obedience of your word. **Lord God of Israel, there is no God like thee, in the heavens above nor in the earth beneath who keepest covenant and mercy with thy servant who walk before thee with all their heart.** Father, I totally submit to your way, your word and your will. My soul says yes! Yes Lord, I'll go as you lead. I'll speak what you say to whomever, whenever and wherever. I will not fear. God, I give you a total and surrendered yes, now and forever more. My soul says yes. Shekinah Glory in my ear... All their songs are so powerful.*

Where you lead, I will follow until the very end. Thank you, Lord for bringing me to a place of complete obedience, predestined and foreordained from the very foundation of the world. Born into the light of your glory, I'll forever seek your face, hear your voice and obey your word. Hallelujah, Jesus. Amen.

Inmate church service was awesome tonight. I was the speaker for this service. We discussed **Ezekiel 3: 17-21, Matthew 6:25-31, Isaiah 40:22, 29-31, and Chapter 41:10**. Additionally, I encouraged the congregation to read the book of Romans one chapter every day and again the next day to dissect it. I encouraged them to read and study as a lifestyle, not just for church service.

April 16, 2017 - I woke up early this morning talking to my father Jehovah. I showered, shampooed, groomed, dressed, made the bed, ate a good breakfast and came back to my desk to write what God had impressed upon me to do.

He asked me to serve 12 people who are indigent. Therefore, Lord, I am seeking your guidance to show me their faces.

In minutes their names were revealed to me. Here are their names and dorm numbers. H-3 – Gerri and Tara H7 – Alysha Flynn H-9 – Sandra Steward H-10 – Helen in the Vet dorm, Riggins H-5 – Betty Wilson H-4 – Maria Hudson H-3 – Galisa Alvesson H-2 – Jordan Greek H-6 – Dawn Kong, H-8 and Charlene Red H – 10 (all the real names have been changed of course).

Is God showing me to have a last summer service here with the people listed? A last supper, showing the love of Christ to those who have no other resources of food or family, to demonstrate to them the true love of God?

Father, I thank you that you're showing me the light of your glory to draw others by your spirit. Amen.

Please read these scriptures and allow for your inner ears to hear:

Proverbs 28:27 – He that giveth unto the poor shall not lack...

Proverbs 11:25 - The liberal soul shall be made fat and he that watereth shall be watered also himself...

Psalms 41:1 – Blessed is he that considerate the poor: The Lord will deliver him in time of trouble. There's so many more I don't have time to locate now.

Another scripture located for next Saturday Lady's Luncheon to lift each other in love is **Luke 14: 12-14 – "Then said he also to him that bade him when thou makest a dinner or a supper. Call neither thy friends nor thy brethren, neither thy kinsmen nor thy rich neighbor. Lest they also bid thee again and recompense be made thee. But, when thou makest a feast, call the poor, the maimed, the lame, the blind and thou shall be blessed. For they cannot recompense thee. For thou shalt be recompensed at the resurrection of the just."**

It's Easter, Resurrection Sunday. I need to call Mom tonight. Free Indeed outside church is coming tonight. The Praise Team is dancing and the choir is singing. I'm looking forward to a glorious night in the Lord. Resting in his presence and meditating in the word. No real movement. In fact, I'm staying in my PJ's until time for dinner. We ate Chinese in the room today. The whole room pitched in noodles with lemon tea sauce and skins.

It's Misty's Birthday in addition to being Easter. So, it's a double dinner celebration. It's now, 6:00 p.m., time to get ready for church. Oh my, Free Indeed didn't make it?

So, I was called to give a prayer and Minister Tammy spoke words of the death, burial and resurrection of Christ. We sang, prayed and had a good evening. Now all I need to do is call my family and wish them a Happy Easter. I look forward to starting classes tomorrow. Good night.

April 17, 2017 – Early class, "Radicals for Christ" 7:30 – 9:00 a.m. taught by Shavonne Giles. It's now back to the basic. I've had this class before with Brunette Nelson and I'm a "seasoned Christian" of many years. But, I can always "renew and refresh." Then my next class is "Coloring Therapy" which takes place at 9:30 – 10:30 a.m. I now have my ear phones on with worship music and am just basking in His glory. Not talking to anyone.

11:00 a.m. – Count, and I slept/napped until 12:30 lunch. At 2:00 p.m., yard call. I walked two miles. I received my store today. I had a snack and now it's time to go to the "Warden's Newsletter" class. Riggins, our Editor and Chief, presented what she had. It sounded so good. We are looking for this newsletter to go into print in May 2017. I pray I won't be here to see it.

Who knows, only God. After class, I went out on the yard to walk some more. This is a great day outside. Thank you, Jesus.

April 18, 2017 - This is another day's journey, another opportunity to get better. The only class I have today is Scrabble club this afternoon and choir rehearsal at 4:40 p.m. I'm going out walking at 9:00 a.m. and 10:30 a.m. I'm walking 25 laps today. Wow! I'm so proud of my consistency.

April 19, 2017– Wow, it's the 19th. It's hard to believe April is almost over. Here's another month almost gone. Jesus is soon to come. Time is drawing nearer than ever before.

It's been a "routine day." I didn't go to lunch or dinner. I rested, read, walked and took Kairos this evening. I spoke to my sister, Cynthia, for a few minutes before I went out to yard call. All is well. I had a snack, watched Greenleaf at 10:00 p.m. and called it a night.

April 20, 2017 – Another day and I'm waking up every thirty minutes (3:00 a.m., again at 3:30 a.m., 4:00 a.m. and again at 4:30 a.m.) But I didn't get up until 5:00 a.m. Of course, I take my shower and groom. It's now 5:20 a.m. It's, time to keep it moving. I'm dressed, grooming is complete, made my bed, cleaned my area and it's now 6:00 a.m. I'm not in the best mood... I guess I was hoping not to still be here. I have told my mind that it's ok. Go back to functioning full blast and don't worry about it. However, it just doesn't want to flee my heart to get out. Nevertheless, "a delay is not a denial," another saying I've heard from the Bishop. Choir rehearsal is at 5:00 p.m.

At 6:00 p.m., there is a new class called, "Anger Management" tonight. It's been an ok day. Tomorrow is Family day and my family will not be here because I thought I'd been gone. Its ok, it's more for kids anyway.

There will be face painting, sack races, Hulu hoop, Bouncy house, kids dance contest, pizza, and ice cream. I'm ok, hallelujah anyway! It's much better than the Run Arounds Family day a few weeks ago. Dedric surprised me and was present; I cannot describe the feeling of Joy that has come over me! A fresh wind.

April 21, 2017 – I wrote a letter to Deputy Warden Hendrix requesting that she finds out why I'm still here. It's been six weeks. Lord, am I not finished with my assignment? What else do I need to do? Please reveal it to me and I will do it. It's been a great day thus far. I made my own buttered grits with cheese crackers. They had eggs and coffee at chow. I wrote letters to Minnie Daniels, Joyce Riley in L.A. and to my sister, Ressie, with a visitation form attached. It's Family day, but of course, my family isn't here only because I thought I wouldn't be here. When I was told about T.C. six weeks ago, I just knew it would be within the first three weeks. Anyway, Ozzie and Gwen are coming to visit me tomorrow and Sunday. So, I'm good. The prison staff showed us a movie called, "Sing," a cute cartoon – a movie with a message of persistence.

April 22, 2017 – It's a great day. A day of visitation from the Lord, my husband Ozzie, and sister Gwen from 9:00 a.m. until 3:00 p.m. They stayed the entire visitation.

What a sacrifice and I am grateful. I've exhausted myself. I'm sleeping until time for church at 6:00 p.m.

7:00 p.m. – Church was great. The spirit of the Lord met us there. **Shake It Off** was my topic tonight. Another story I heard at one of the Word of Faith services. It's a story of a farmer trying to bury his old washed up donkey. He dug a hole and threw the donkey in the hole. Every time the farmer threw a shovel full of dirt in the hole to bury him, the donkey would shake it off and step on it, packing the dirt down under his feet until so much dirt was thrown and packed under his feet that he eventually rose to the top and walked away from the hole. Now that's a place to shout, right here!

You and I are not washed up because we are in prison. We can shake it off and step out! Every time someone tells you "you're nothing", shake it off. "You're a jail bird," shake it off, "you're a has been," shake it off, "a felon," SHAKE IT OFF and put it under your feet, and eventually, you'll be able to walk away into your destiny! Praise God Hallelujah!!!!!

I went back to the dorm at 9:00 p.m. for count. 9:30 p.m., I watched a movie called, "Sing." Then I called Ozzie and Gwen to thank them for coming. I then called Cynthia and mom. It's 10:15 p.m. now. I'm about ready for bed. I read myself to sleep.

April 23, 2017 – Wow, what a revelation God has shown me this morning. Last night I completed a book by the wife of Evangelist Perry Stone, an "Israel Preacher." Pam Stone shares her life as the wife of international minister and shares stories about her husband. It is very interesting and eye opening for me. For a season during the incarceration, God had instructed me to read <u>only my bible</u> and to stop reading other "helpful" books. God wanted to show me through His word what he wanted me to know and to do. I obeyed God and denied myself other books I had the opportunity to read. Now, I've got it. A doer of his word and complete obedience has brought me to the revelation of this situation in my life. Lord, thank you for the divine revelation. You could have allowed me to stay in my flesh. However, you looked past my ignorance and showed me more.

I was bringing stress and strife on unnecessarily and talking the word, but not actually walking it out! ***To thine own self be true.*** I'm thinking about my sister Gwen and my husband Ozzie. There are so many things I don't like about either of them. (I'm sure there's things about me they don't like either.) I even said to myself and probably

Page 160

should not say this aloud. Yes, I have been told "I talk too much" and that's self-evident now. I thought to myself (as he pushed her in her wheel chair and she's holding his walker entering into the visitation room coming to see me after driving two and a half hours), "they should be coupled together with all their "ailments." I was sort of "embarrassed." Gwen is super friendly and just talking up a storm to people like she knows them, *proudly* telling them "that's my sister."

Now, as I allowed God to "work on me" I had to come to realize, what if it was me? What would I want people to feel about me if I was on a walker? How would I feel if the shoe was on the other foot? I have a co-laborer in the gospel, a nurse who has a husband with a trach/voice box who doesn't speak clearly. He's visibly handicapped. She cares for him and speaks to him as a proud loving wife. What an example! She is a living epistle that the word speaks about, not preaching it, but she's living it by example.

I feel ashamed. Here I am a woman of God with all these words in my mouth and say "I'm concerned." But honestly, I am feeling like I'm almost "too good for him."

If God can take the mouth of a donkey to speak, surely, he can use my husband and develop him for his purpose. I can pray, under girt him as a help mate, and work with him in our home. I can fix the right meals to encourage him to lose the weight, speak wisdom and kind words. I can support him to develop him, to become the intellectual man he and I both can be proud of. Admittedly again, I was afraid for him to talk to my "intellectual" friends, as I think about his limited vocabulary. Although my husband doesn't speak with the lingo of a business man, he is not lazy and will do everything he can to help me. When his health allowed, he would cut the grass, clean out the culverts dammed up by the beavers under our driveway, fixed things in the home; to my surprise, he recently changed the thermostat which saved money from me calling an HVAC technician.

Osvaldo is excellent with his computer skills; he speaks Spanish fluently, and could be an interpreter if he wanted to. He's not the president of a company, a physician, a stock broker, or a big preacher who can use "big" intellectual words, but he has so many other wonderful qualities that meet my needs. He cooks, clean, wash and fold clothes better than I do. He serves my plate to me when he cooks. Intimacy has always been 100% from day one, so I really have no reason to complain. I know he loves me and he sometimes attends M.A.S.S. (men after spiritual strength) so he's getting some of Bishop's wisdom.

He's no razor scholar, but I'm not the sharpest knife in the drawer either. He may not be everything I want, (physically) but he is everything I need (emotionally). This is not all about me, but it's about the will of the father. It's me walking out this word and doing what thus saith the Lord in the ministry. Why did I wait until I was almost at husband number five before I figured this out? Nevertheless, I got it now. Jesus take the wheel. I can't wait until my husband comes back on tomorrow. I will apologies for my thoughts and telling him how I feel/felt about him. Because I'm going to say this by the leading of the Holy Spirit; I know he will be "ok" after our talk.

I just remembered a quote from Bishop Bronner. He said, *"Change the way you look at things, and the things you look at will change."*

As I am writing this book you are currently reading, my editor asked me if I wanted to re-consider and take what I'm telling you here about my husband out of the book; I said no, absolutely not. I want to be totally transparent, and allow God to deliver me from how I feel. This will be a testimony to God's power and glory in changing me. **Proverbs 14:1 says every wise woman buildeth her house: but the foolish plucketh it down with her hands***.*

April 24, 2017 – This is another day that the Lord has made. **"I will rejoice and be glad in it."** Another opportunity to get it right! God is so good and faithful to me. My husband and sister Gwen are coming to visit again today. It's a Monday State Holiday and feels like a Saturday.

11:00 a.m. Count. - I was called out to the visitation area. My family, Ozzie and Gwen were the only ones who came to visit at the entire prison today. I felt so special. We had the entire Visitation room and vending machines to ourselves. They brought two rolls of quarters. I ate two packages of Buffalo Spicy Hot wings, (four tiny pieces each package), Lays chips, a Carrot cake and sprite. I was encouraging Ozzie and Gwen with the word God gave me. I tearfully allowed the Lord to have his way in breaking me. We actually had a very good visitation. Later in the evening, I spoke to my sister in the Lord, Paula Cook. She shared with me all the Lord had given to her for her 3:00 p.m. deliverance message. It was wonderful. I love it when we share our words from the Lord with each other. My sister, Cynthia, makes this all possible doing a three-way call from her phone. Thanks baby sis.

Tonight, its BBQ chicken night and I've got two pieces, a leg and thigh combo X2. It tasted so good. I couldn't eat anything else. In fact, I'm not eating anything else until breakfast. I had a shower, did a little reading and had a good night sleep.

Lord, thank you for this day. I pray your perfect will be done in me, with me and through me for your glory. Amen.

April 25, 2017 – 4:30 a.m. - Up as usual with my routine. Dressed and laid back down until breakfast. I had grits, sausage, potatoes and coffee. I then slept until 8:00 a.m. count. I went back to sleep until 9:00 a.m. I went on my "Wellness walk."

10:30 a.m. - I drunk a cup of coffee trying to wake up. I also wrote in my journal and read ten chapters in my bible. I e-mailed my sister Judy from the church. I'm now going to meditate in God's presence until he speaks. Lunch is the next actual thing on today's schedule. We had Peanut Butter sandwiches, soup and squash or were those rutabagas? For dessert, we had bread pudding which I don't eat. I rested, then I wrote to sister Roz. Actually, it's Pastor Rosalyn Durham from the Sword of the Lord Ministries. A "son" of the prophet Bro. Randy. She is so anointed and powerful in the Lord!

Hey, store is here! I didn't even notice as I had my ear bubs in listening to glorious gospel music as I wrote. Once store has been put away, it's now time for dinner. We had meat patty with rice and gravy, beans and cornbread. I don't eat beans at all. I ate only half my meal then headed back to the dorm. I had fifteen-minute rest and knew it was time for Choir rehearsal. I heard church called to sign out. Although we didn't go far, any movement from one area to another, we still had to sign out when leaving the dorm. Highway to Hedges ministry is here. They're not my favorite. (They don't believe in women preachers) However, anytime I have an opportunity to hear praise, even if it's country, and hear the word of God, even if it's elementary, it gets me out of the dorm and gives me something to do until evening.

Less than a dozen inmates showed up. I guess no one else cares much for this ministry either. Well, let's see what God does!

April 26, 2016 – Good morning Jesus. "I'm so glad you're here. You bring joy bells when you are near, lift all my burdens, lift all my fears, good morning Jesus, so glad you're here." Songs of praise, I love Jesus. He my savior, when storms are raging, he's my shelter, where he leads me, I will follow, I love Jesus, he loves me.

4:30 a.m. – I showered, groomed, dressed and rested.

5:30 a.m. – I hear a stir. There's a shakedown going on.

All the inmates are scattering like roaches when you turn on a kitchen light at night. I've got nothing to hide. So, it doesn't matter if they come into my locker or not. I'm good. A shakedown is when the guards randomly come into the dorm and "toss" all your stuff, and I don't mean gently either.

The next morning, they had cold grits, hard rubbery sausage patties, peaches and bread with pieces of peaches baked in it.   I'm going to read my bible and wait to hear from God. Oh Lord, here goes my Nay Sayers.

A fool is known by a multitude of words. There are so many of these loose - lip females talking too much. I am now ready for inspection. But I'm going out on the yard to walk.

9:00 – 10:45 a.m. – I almost walked six miles. I'm soaking wet from sweat. I freshened up, changed all my clothes and rested until lunch.   At lunch, we had Bologna, sliced cucumbers, and potatoes salad.   I napped all the way till dinner time, and then played Scrabble until church service. Now, I'm sitting here waiting for the Lord to come forth.   The Atkinson Ministry is here tonight.

April 27, 2017 – 3:30 a.m. and my roomie's packing up with the officers to be transferred to T.C. I'm not going today? I've e-mailed my husband and son to ask them both to contact someone to find out why I'm still here. I'm pretty sure that there are so many more that need to go to T.C. way more than I do. So, I'm going to just relax and let it go.

I signed up for another class today. I took my blood pressure medication, something I didn't have before prison. I ate, slept and tried to be merry. Of course, I'll continue in the word of God through ministry music and worshipping God on a daily basis.

I still journal daily and will complete the next series of Highway to Hedges Bible study course. Thank God it's as well as it is. I walked five – six miles at breakneck speed with a girl next door, Sandra. I went to rest and then had lunch. We were served Spaghetti and turnip greens. Next, I cleaned up my locker, talked with associates and before I knew it, it was dinner time. After dinner, I went to Kairos.

There was some excitement in the air because a new group of participants are going in Kairos as table angels, spiritual waitresses, as they call us. The guards are checking everybody in. Once they're all in the gym, we collect the left overs and trash. I colored place mats for tomorrow meals and just assisted with the set-up of chairs for chapel tomorrow as well. Now, I'm done. I'm going to work on my Bible study.

April 28, 2017 – Its 6:30 a.m. and for some reason, I thought it was Saturday. I had to jump up, quickly shower and get my clothes outside the door for laundry pickup. The Lord reminded me I was fasting for the Mighty Men of Valor conference, for Brother Michael and Sister Judy Jackson's ministry. So, thank you Jesus. I'll eat on my word and Bible study all day until after the conference in Newnan, at The Sword of the Lord. Sister Judy Jackson's husband, Mike, is teaching a powerful word today, I'm sure. While I'm e-mailing Judy, I heard the words, "tell Mike to prepare expecting God to move in Power, Purpose and Position." He is really going to show himself strong.

I'm having my spiritual breakfast in my bible, getting into my word now and spending all day with Jesus. It's been peace alone time with the Lord. Later, I go into the Day room.

At 5:00 p.m., I called Cynthia to inquire about my food and clothing package. However, I was interrupted by someone who wants to talk or shall I say, "complain/gossip." I listened, but it began to affect my spirit after being full of the Spirit of God all day. To have someone dump trash into my clean spirit was just not going to work today. I soon removed myself.

Later between 5:00 and 6:00 p.m., I was sitting at the table where some Spade players had been. They were missing a player and I "decided" to play since I was sitting there. There's nothing wrong with it, but people who'd NEVER seen me play cards were in shock. It wasn't the time after being in God's presence all day in the word and fasting with prayer. The Bible says to shun the very appearance of evil, right? Cards are not sinful, but it's the cursing, language, attitude, cheating, etc. that sometimes comes along with the card playing that makes on lookers question the situation.

6:00 p.m. and Kairos number ten walk is going to take place. I participated in number nine walk four months ago. I remembered what an awesome experience it was. They are eating good food and I want some. I'm about to break my fast. It's after 6:00 p.m., but I couldn't get into the kitchen for the topping on my potatoes. I already have Idaho mash potatoes packets in my locker. However, my potatoes here have broccoli salad with raisins, bacon bits and Balsamic Vinaigrette dressing. Yum! Always temptation, Lord, I thank you all is well as it is. I'm going back into my bible studies and rest with you! Your word is yea and Amen. Thank you for this day. I'm recognizing that I have an "issue" with food. Lord I need deliverance!

April 29, 2017 – Thank you Lord for another day that you have made. **"I will rejoice and be glad in it."** It's my day to clean the bathroom and get T.V. I'll be the one holding the remote control!

8:00 a.m. - Count Time. I am all done with breakfast, and it was great. I had scrambled eggs, grits, pancakes, diced potatoes, a banana and coffee.

I ate 100 percent of the food. I took my shower, ice cooler filled and I'm ready to just get into my bible study again. They can have the remote. I'm hanging out with Jesus.

CHAPTER 8

TRANSFER TO METRO TRANSITION CENTER (M.T.C.)

May 1, 2017 – I'm waking up having some kind of day, feeling some kind of way.

While standing in line to sign out for wellness walk, I walked into the bubble and told the officers "put handcuffs on me and take me into lock down." I wasn't smiling. She didn't take me seriously. So, I said, "Ok, you've been warned. When you find that I've busted somebody's head against this cement wall and they ask you why, you can say I warned you." I signed out and went outside to walk in the yard. After about 30 minutes, I get called into the Deputy Warden's office. She asked me "what's going on with you"? The Warden, Unit Manager and Captain are all there and I tell them, "I'm tired of prison and I'm ready to go. Let me out of here. I need new scenery. I asked to be moved now. I'm sick of my roommates; these silly young females are getting to be too much." Deputy Grier sees the serious threat of my desire and says to the guard, "move her immediately." Go back to your room with Captain Sody with a cart and pack up all your stuff." I was placed in A30. "Great, I feel better already."

After dinner and a shower at 9:00 p.m. count took place. The entire dorm prayed together, read scripture and one lady sang a song she wrote, taught us and we all joined in. What a glorious evening. After the news went off, I went to sleep and the next thing I knew, I'm tapped at 2:30 a.m. with two large trash bags with an officer saying "pack it up!" Glory hallelujah. I'm being transferred to the T.C. Finally, it's been so long and I can't wait. I was packed in ten minutes waiting at the door to be bussed out! Thank you, Jesus for all that you have done for me today and always. There were four or five of us loaded up on the van to go. Two were dropped at Pulaski state prison and the rest of us were brought to the Metro Transitional center in Atlanta. I arrived at M.T.C. on Tuesday, May 2, 2017, approximately at **11:00 a.m**. - The long-term residents unpacked my inventory for check in and re-packed my stuff. I was taken to room C-359 and given the bottom bunk, my roommate's name was Gloria and two others whose names I can't remember. She was there speaking with two friends. I tossed my bags into the locker and went to change out. I'm so tired. I laid on top of the mat and slept.

Thank God the laundry lady, Ms. Williams, is cool. She replaced my old soiled mat and both jump suits which now fit better.

Ms. Nelson, my friend from E.W.F saw me and came to greet me. She introduced me to two spiritual sisters. Later, after dinner, she and I went outside to walk around the building. Then I had a Bible study with women in transition. However, I was too exhausted to participate long. I left at 7:30 p.m. and went to bed. I was knocked out until 9:00 p.m. count. Then Nelson texted Cynthia to let her know that I was here and that I needed some money. Yep, we can have cell phones in the M.T.C.

May 3, 2017 – I'd just made a bowl of grits when I was called to go and see Assistant Superintendent Lofton in the "A building" for an intake interview. I sat the bowl of grits on the top shelf inside of my locker. I headed up to Building A and shared a great first-time meeting with Ms. Lofton. I was able to share my frustrations and release anxieties. Her only rule was, "DON'T LIE TO ME".

On my return to my room, it was time for inspection and I had no time to eat my grits. I'm so hungry because I slept through breakfast. I was just so tired.

My locker is a hot mess. What happened next? The Superintendent came straight into my locker. The first thing she picks up is my bowl of grits as I explained to her what happened. Superintendent Wiggin's also commented on how much groceries I had.

Again, I tried to explain how I was informed that I would not be able to "shop" for thirty days. Therefore, I needed to have enough food to eat for a month. Then Chief Jackson asked," how did you know you were coming as it's a breach of security to tell you before you arrive?." I told her, as soon as I knew I was approved, back in March, I began buying and putting back food. The Superintendent laughed and said, I'm going to call Warden McMillian and let her know to tell her people to stop those tales. It doesn't take a month to get food. In fact, you can get a package after being here ten days." I replied, "But its personal hygiene products and coffee, not food, not to exceed ten pounds." right? Or at least that's what I'm told via (inmate.com). They left me alone and allowed me to keep all of my stuff, however; I must rearrange everything to fit neater in a horseshoe style, where she can step her foot into the locker.

Not having been here 48 hours yet, I'm called out in the am to go to Building A to see my counselor, Mr. Johnson. He told me, "It's all good, 100 percent". There is a ninety day early release possibility (called clemency) which would mean October, 2018. Can be my release date as long as I do what I'm supposed to and have no DR's (Disciplinary reports).

I spent time walking the yard around the building at least an hour, as I enjoyed doing at E.W.F. Residents here are sent out onto the yard as punishment for smoking in the bathroom, not as a pleasurable experience as it was at E.W.F. This location has no fences; buses pull right up onto the property. If you escape, you will be caught and five to ten year will be added to your sentence. Later, I go into my room and begin to write what God is downloading into my spirit. I'm open to do whatever it is God has me here for.

I need a five-page biography to turn into the Classification Committee in thirty days. It's already done, Hallelujah! I'm given my computation report which says six Pic Points applied. So, instead of two years now, it's showing 18 month which would be October 11, 2018. But I'm informed once I've done my 30 - day classification, I have to do 160 hours of community service in order to classify and be given employment. I could possibly go home on early release and once probation is "satisfied", I could be off paper in two years. Thank you, Jesus!

A one - page essay of what I've returned to M.T.C. has to be written and given to my counselor after 30 days so that I can move into the next phase. What's next? "<u>A man can never discover new islands if he's afraid of losing sight of the shore.</u>" I believe I hear God speaking a career in law/politics and there may be a door opening for a position at the Governor's office I'm told. Ms. Promise, the Employee Coordinator will be calling me out after Mr. Johnson speaks on my behalf.

After my 30 days in the M.T.C., all I need is for my husband to retrieve my Social Security Card and Birth Certificate. I need for him to bring it here on this Sunday; I cannot pursue employment without it.

Thank you, Father, I was able to complete my ten-day package form and my counselor signed off on it. He said that he will give it to the chief to sign off on then will give it back to me to mail to Paula so she can pick up the items and mail it here. I'm glad my visitors don't need to drive three hours now. It is only about 20 to 30 minutes for them to come visit me at this M.T.C.

I'm expecting Ozzie and Gwen Sunday. They can bring my Social Security Card and Birth Certificate. In addition, they can take some of these books home and that will help me open up room in my locker.

I plan to get my hair done next week. My counselor allowed me to come back the next day and speak to him regarding working with the staff here. My counselor told me, "You are too intelligent and too smart to be working at McDonald's or a Chicken house." No offense to those who do work there.

Ms. Promise informed me that I could work with Ms. Robinson, the GED teacher or teach C.P.R., First Aid and Positive Speaking. My counselor will make the connection. I'm happy to be out of prison but, still not off the radar just yet. God is not through with me yet.

However, it won't be long, Hallelujah. Job readiness is the first of several classes I need to complete within the next thirty days.

Below are all the new rules I had to learn at this new location in order for me to meet all the requirements for transitioning: *For those who really want to know.*

__Warning: The next 20 pages are the rules and details, the do's and don'ts of EVERYTHING (don't fall asleep or you could skip over 20 pgs.& read the rest of my story)__

May 5, 2017 - This is what I've learned so far:

- **Count:** Midnight, 5:00 a.m., 6:00 a.m., Noon, 4:00 p.m., 6:00 p.m. and 9:30 p.m.

- **Details:** In House (See Schedules).

- **Staff:** On your feet, stand at attention until told to carry on by security and learn the rules with handbook which gave you the **Do's and Don'ts of the program.**

- **Work Release** – It is a privilege earned. I am still in the custody of the Department of Corrections.

- **$200** – The dollar amount charged to you, your account, if you try to escape, if there was a warrant, or you had to be returned to prison, and if they had to use maximum security. You will also add five to ten years to your sentence.

- **Security** – Sign in/out, call in if you are going to be late returning back to the center, have a legal matter, accident or contact with the police.

- **Cell Phones** – Clear cover, no ear buds with speaking capabilities, take mic out. The counselor must approve phone slip. First, family must have it activated before it arrives. The phone must always be on vibrate, text and talk quiet. Never lend phone to anyone or it will be taken.

- **Financials** – Can make withdrawal for two reasons

- To pay cell phone bill

- To buy special needs. Receipts are required - special, property purchased. You cannot use this money to purchase food. Anything above $5.00 must be returned to the Business office.

- **Contrabands** – Any items with alcohol or any excessive unapproved items.

- **Food:** Cannot bring it in from anywhere. Only what's on the approved sheet can be purchased and brought in with receipt, unless family buys it, and it must always be approved before bringing it in. Even if family pays. My $$ = my receipt. Lunch/outside food cannot be brought back after work.

- **Phone:** 7'screen with Pandora, U-tube, NETFLIX, clear case ok, NO FACEBOOK.

- **Forms** – Hair products and medications require a special form to be signed off on.

- **One Monthly Package form** – This form must be given to the counselor by the fifth of each month and post marked by the last day of the month.

- **Items and Quantity Permitted:** You must have a clear pouch.

- **Make up**: One of each of the following – eyeliner, foundation, press powder, eye shadow, four colors, eye brow pencil, mascara and blush. You can have two lipsticks.

- **Toiletries** – Baby lotion, Baby powder, Baby oil, Shampoo/Conditioner (2 each), Deodorant (2), Hair Moisturizers, Setting Lotion, Setting Gel (1 each) Toothbrush – Oral B, Toothpaste – No alcohol, Washing Powder (22 Load limit) no liquid or pods (zip lock bag it).

- **Batteries** – For remote, clock, watch, etc. Limited to 12 total - (AA, AAA, D, D. 9 volt regular)

- **Writing Materials**– Non-retractable, clear- blue or black (2 only), pencils, pens, Magazines and book (2), Photo albums, 10 Pictures limit, Plastic not metal binder. Walkman or MP3 Player (1) 1 clear 6 - inch Purse/clutch. 200 sheet notebook paper, or 4 legal pads

- **Jewelry From Home** – (1) Watch, (1) Neckless with religious pendent only, (2) Pair earrings, small – No dangling, no post, no clips on and one wedding ring.

- **Clothes allowed - This is what I'm able to bring back from my golden pass home once I "classify"**

(2) Bath towels – Solid color (Color fast)

(4) Wash Clothes – (14) hangers (Black or white)

(1) Belt – Black/Brown, reversible

(5) Shoes – Boots, Tennis, work, slippers, and shower shoes

(7) Pair Socks – Scarfs (2) Head/Neck

(4) T-Shirts – White only, no pockets (under garments) No tank tops

T-Shirt – Color with pockets (outer garment)

(2) Gym Shorts – Knee Length only

(2) Thermal Underwear – (2) sets

(2) Sweater/or sweat shirt (1) each No zipper, no hood

(1) Slips – Whole or half (only 1 not both)

(6) Pants (4) of these (2) Dresses

(6) Blouses (6) outfits, (1 Pants Suits = (1) = one outfit

(10) Panties

(7) Bras – White, no underwire

(1) Coat or Jacket (No Hoods) (1) pair of Gloves

(1) Girdle

(1) Jogging Suit * Separate from 6 outfits?

(2) Knee Highs

(2) Panty Hose

(2) Pajama - Solid color

(1) Knit Skull Cap – Plain

- **Food Items**

Coffee – 16 oz. Jar/Box (Instant)

Soda – Six pack, Powder drink mix – (20 oz. or less) Water or Juice

Sugar or Sweetener – 50 – 100 package limits

Creamer – Powder, 50 – 100 limit or (Liquor -22 oz.)

Hard Candy – 2 packages – 1 lb. bags – Individually wrapped – 2 bag limits

Trail Mix or nuts – 6 small individual bags

Chips/or Popcorn, 6 small boxes or 1-24 bags variety pack of chips

14 – Dry Soup mix/complete meals – 14 oz. chunk cups

8 – Cereal – Hot/Cold – Individual boxes/packets – Single serving size

8 – Fruit Cups Breakfast bars or Pop tarts (Box of 6)

6 pack – Snack Cakes or Cookies or Crackers (1 box) – Individually wrapped

1 Salt, 1 Pepper, 1 Hot Sauce, 1 seasoning – **Plastic** jar – small

SCHEDULES

This was my personal schedule Monday

– Women of Wisdom – 6:30 p.m.

Tuesday – Women in Transition – 6:30 p.m.

Wednesday – Whatever church service came in

Thursday – Job Readiness – Class Room (1) – 3:30 – 5:30 p.m.

Friday - Women in Transition – 10:30 a.m.

Consumer Education – 2:00 – 3:00 p.m.

World of Work -Business – 6:30 p.m.

Saturday and Sunday - 9:00 – 1:00 p.m., visitation of family and friends

Saturday/Sunday Worship – 6:30 – 8:00 p.m.

Up and Dressed by 5"30 a.m.

Up for Inspection ready by 7:00 am – 4:30 p.m. – Monday – Friday

No T.V. Lounges until after 4:30 p.m. or 1:30 Weekends

Sleep 8 hours – 7 days a Week

Detail done by 7:30 a.m. on Weekdays at 9:00 a.m. on Weekends

Job Description – By 8:30 p.m. If I didn't have a detail, you remained in room until details completed by others.

Wednesday – Laundry sheets/Thursday Clothes (2X weeks only)

No Open Containers. No room mingling, no eating in room

T.V.'s clocks, fans on top of lockers

Meals – Breakfast – 5:00 – 6:00 a.m., Lunch – 12 – 1:00 and Dinner 4:00 – 6:00 p.m.

Check Bulletin Board for Schedule and Details

Pack Lunch to take to work pack-out) = Bologna sandwich, Orange, and Cake

All policies had to be learned, and recited to the committee to qualify to go on pass.

EMPLOYMENT POLICY – A PRIVILEGE/ Not a right.
(You can be sent back to prison to complete your
sentence if you don't follow the rules)

- Must ride Marta to and from job – No exception

- Must go to and from work w/o any deviation

- Cannot ride at work with other employees unless approved by Supervisor

- Must not inform friend/family of place of employment

- Must not meet anyone to and from work (no escort) – this is considered an unauthorized meeting

- Must have pay check, direct deposit or mailed to T.C. by employer

- Must turn in all tips to center

- Must work under legal name and note T.C. as legal residence

- Must allow all deductions Federal and state, anything else must be authorized and approved (health benefits)

- Must eat in Employee's Break room only – Do not leave work for lunch

- **SCHEDULE DAY HOURS**

- Must inform Ms. Promise, Employment Manager of any status change in employment.

- Must not accept anything from anyone for any reason unless approved.

- Must receive approval from Employment Manager to attend lunches.

- Training on property – Who will submit request to classes?

- All Scheduled Days off, OT, must be approved.

- Work after 10 p.m. = sleep in day time = 1-hour arrival back into the center allowed to sleep 8 hours, then still must get up and do details and attend classes.

- Room and Board = 30 percent of your Net earnings, not to exceed $90.00 a week.

T and I = Transportation and incidents $10 -$25 – or $55.00/week (based on your status, unemployed, in job search, or actively employed).

$10.00 Un-employed - $25.00 classified and in job search, $55.00 employed.

But you must have more than $300.00 in your account to get $55.00.

Special W/D by 8:00 a.m. on Thursdays – Request must be submitted to counselor and supervisor must approve and must have approval balance to make the W/D receipts for whatever purchased with special funds must be turned in to security officer with a receipt.

- **CHARGES**

Taken FROM YOUR MTC ACCOUNT a DR (Disciplinary report) $200.000 Unauthorized absence from the center, and/or positive alcohol breathalyzer, ($100) and Drug Screen ($200.00 fine)

Damage to state property – Restitution

- **ALL**

Passes, Phase Movements, Incentives,

Supervisors can extend-Special leave to residents who meet/Exceed Performance Standards

Increase Family and Community contact – Smoother transition into home

Plus, an incentive for positive behavior or adjustment

Compassion leave – Medical leave

- **WEEKLY**

Passes Earned with Demonstrations of Satisfactory Program Performance

Missing classes, work, and noncompliance with rules can forfeit passes

- **EVERY WEEK**

Phase I = P 30 days = 6 hours of "informed" freedom – up to 30 miles each way

Phase II = P 60 days = 9 hours home pass = up to 60 miles away

Phase III = p 90 days=12 hours home pass – up to 100 miles away

Complete Pass Application in Blue/Black ink *legibly * Phase

Edith Mae Page – 1001747907 – Employment

Location/Length of time on job

Date _____ Time_____ requesting for pass

- **RESTRICTIONS for Passes**

ONLY 8:00 a.m. − 8:00 p.m. −   Maximum time allowed away from the center

Must be an immediate family member, with complete address 0000 Brownville Road, Powder Spring, GA 30127, and phone no# (000) 000-0000

Supervisor will verify landline to be assured that enough time has been requested to ensure adequate travel time to return to the center on time − May be modified if necessary)

Submit Pass request to counselor no later than 8:00 a.m. Mondays

Must carry Pass Authorization on person while out on Pass

Must submit Pass to Correctional officer upon returning and sign in/search

Must go to designated place stated on Pass only − If not, Pass Privilege can be revoked. If/or late return as well.

Phone must not ring up to 10 times or D.R. disciplinary report will result! If you do not answer phone, you will automatically lose next pass

C.O. can call again to verify you are there – Home

No restaurant, No movie theater, No place except home

Copy and drop pay stub in Business Office Box or you will not receive T and I

- **SHOPPING PASSES**

All items must be listed on back of shopping pass and accompanied with a receipt that shows item, amount and location of where you shopped - Cash only. Any deviation from this is considered contraband and will be taken.

Visitors Allowed – 12 Total, Family and 2 significant others

Special Visits – Must be approved by Classification committee

NO ONE can visit, Monday – Friday – 8:00 a.m. – 4:30 p.m., unless approved. Must request 24 hours in advance

Superintendent must approve Clergy Visit

Chaplain = Pastoral care, workshop services, support, crisis intervention and community volunteer = Weekly orientation

Classes = to create positive atmosphere in attitude to live a crime free productive life.

Cognitive reconstruction – 30 days – 30 classes total

Classification Committee = phase movement up to 30 days work assignment

   = Approve/disapprove request from residents

Library = A quiet area can be set aside on a regular basis for studying and business reading

*Submit in writing request to the counselor to receive approved time for use of the Public Law Library

You need a pass to go to the Local Library – the Superintendent will ensure 2 hours/week.

1, 2 and 3 Phase System:

- Counselor submits request for advancement to Classification committee

- A.D.R. (Disciplinary report) will set you back 30 days

Personality – Orientation/Assessment to Prep for Phase 1

Phase 1 is a matter of timing, 160 hours of community services

I'm doing my work detail – But these classes they offer; I could teach - nevertheless, it's a means to an end so I will sit in them all and participate

(4) – Budgeting – Consumer Education (Money Management)

(4) – Employment – Job Readiness – (How to get and hold a job

(2) – Learning – Electives (2) RT Whatever you need/want

Detour

GED/ABE/Matrix, NA, AA – As required R/t Substance Abuse P 30 days – June 7, 2017 – Wednesday

(I didn't have to take any of this)

* – Good Attitude and volunteering

* - Completed forms turned into counselor

- Required Signatures – Chaplin Orientation

MOU: - Memo of Understanding – Security Orientation

Checklist complete (with Social Security on file – Counselor Orientation 5/5

Purchase Marta Card

Phase 1 Movement:

- 5 or more pages Biography – Locate and maintain employment 30 days

- Individual Counseling – Employment Counseling

- House detail – am/pm – 1 Elective/group

Job search July 5 = 6 Hour Pass – Weekly

Employed August 5 = 30 days = Prep for Phase II Movement – Attitude and Progress = 9 hours Passes/week

Phase 1 = June 14 July 14 = 30 days

– September 14 – July 5

-August 5 - September/October= Home for Thanksgiving (I'd hope, but I had to work.)

Phase II Movement: 9 Hour/60 Mile limit

*Stabilized Employment October 14 = 60 days from

-Complete Essay; 1 page what I gave back to M.T.C.

_Continue House Detail – a.m./p.m. -Reflect my purpose, feelings, dreams, and goals.

-Individual and Employment Counseling   Re: Family, Self and Significant other

-1 Elective Class/Group -30   Hours   of   Community Service

*Demonstrate Initiative and Creativity

60 days from the date, I moved into Phase II

July - August 30   August - September

30 =   Now ready

        *Release Preparation - *

-Essay, how I have benefited from M.T.C.

-Project, make a speech/hold a forum r/t my interest at a house meeting

-Coordinate a great speaker to make a presentation for the T.C.

Phase 3 Movement: = 12 Hour Passes - 100 Mile Limit

-Renew Georgia Driver License --Individual   and Employment Counseling

-Maintain Stable Employment - and   House Detail

-Formulate A Release Plan –and complete a final group

*Outside Activities with staff

Accredited College

Outside Activities Passes for medical, school and other appointments

*** After I'm classified: Submit to Counselor Johnson

- Completely and thoroughly filled out application for Activity Pass to attend church (not related to 6 Hour Pass)

- Submit Hair modification form – get the gray out! (Denied, "changes my identity")

- Complete form to approve cell phone – Phone See that Sgt. M. Jones needs to release phone to be engraved with name and GDG number

- In addition to everything, on the back of the Golden Pass

  -This was my first shopping experience since incarceration; what was I going to do with my limited time and money?

  *Walmart (inside store) – Eye glass? Change frames

  Family paying for all – Mani and Pedi – w/time frame

Family shop — While I receive services to make time frame work.

MODIFIED ITEMS

- Candy — not individually wrapped (entire content Ziploc)

- Maple Peanut Cluster — or small plastic bottle Maple syrup

-Clear zippers pouch 6X4 — clutch, but, w/strap/should carry

T& I = transportation & incidentals = $10.00/0 Wait till $25.00 Job

Between Friday and Saturday — Sign Book — Pick up on Wednesday

Food and money = matching receipts, purchase what you list and have money for.

-Special W/D — Receipts of shopping

-White Pass = Receipts of shopping

-Home Pass = Home only; No shopping

-Activity Pass = Church, Restaurant, and back

? — Box of Envelopes and postage meter stamped envelopes

In addition to approved items – substitution-? Here was my personal list of questions that accompanied my pass request.

Can I bring items from home that listed on Golden Pass like Tennis Shoes?

$55 must have receipt – But- I already have tennis and don't need to buy – so, I'll have no receipt – is that ok?

-Any forms ok'ed, - May I keep copies on my possession?

-Girdle = Body Magic Girdle from home

-Dress = (2) Skirt and Jacket = 1 dress

-Watch – Necklace with cross

-Breakfast bars/Pop tarts – I don't eat?   Can I have Granola Bars?

May 9, 2017 - Ms. Brown Cook Business Orientation Ms. Rivers at **12:30 p.m.**

- All Money orders and paychecks are posted upon receipt

  -Money is not on your account until the business offices gives you a receipt

- T & I = Transportation and Incidentals

-Pay checks are on hold for 14 days after posted in Business office

-Stubs are to be placed into P.O. Box to post to your account

-30% of net earnings and mandatory taxes are the only thing that's taken out; if anything, else comes out, Insurance etc. That is added back into the net earnings.

-Special w/d is approved by Superintendent only – Counselor sheet, it should only be for something special only

-It needs to be for you and your child – cell phone bill (copy of bill must accompany for money)

-Sign T and I Book every Monday – by 6:00 a.m. – No exception*

-Distributions of T and I are in the B.O.

-Escound Fee of $200 goes on hold from your Pay Check

Indigent Loans is for Marta only; not vending machines

1:30 p.m.   Chaplin Orientation – Ms. Sinkfield Not an

employee of G.D. C. – Hart bound

Ministries Children Center 1-3

Only 2 T.C. for Women – Work your Program and you'll be fine

A step closer to home – 90 days-Then get what you want

-Suitable Housing – Apartments – Furnished by ministries – complete

-Support System – Women in transition partnering on outside

-6:30 p.m. Tuesday, Friday @ 10:00 – 12:00 now

Blessed are the flexible, for they shall not be bent out of shape!

May 10, **2017** – Jesus, Jesus, Jesus, what a wonder you are. All day long I've been with Jesus and what a glorious day it has been. I worked all day long. I ate breakfast and worked the kitchen detail. Then, I did my special detail at Helms. This is the prison for pregnant women next door from 9:00 a.m. until 3:00 p.m. There was movement all day. Dinner is from 4:00 p.m. – 6:00 p.m. I'm exhausted. There's my friend Ms. Nelson, and once I'm done with mopping the floor and completing the forms for my Golden Pass Celebration next month, I know I'll be too tired to hang out with her to talk. After my shower, its 9:00 p.m., I going to bed and taking the day off tomorrow. I am going to read rest and relax. No detail for me on Thursday – Hallelujah.

May 11, 2017 – I got up and showered, dressed and read my bible. I was sleeping and there was an inspection. I waited around to be called to get my hair done. I met with friends and ate a hotdog with cheese, chili and corn chips with Nelson and Eterica. Then here comes the stylist into the chow hall to get me. I'm getting a nice short cut, relaxer, and wrapped. I'm back in my room resting while everyone else is out on yard call. I'm so tired. I know I over did it yesterday.

3:30 p.m. – "Job Readiness" Class time – 4:30 p.m. chow time. Let me grab my Sweet Baby Rays sauce for my hamburger and hotdog. Out of this hot jumpsuit and into my shorts. I am now writing out my invitations for my Golden Pass Home visit for June 17, 2017. This is the Lords doing and it's marvelous in my eyes.

All the legal pads are gone for detail journaling. I'm going to find more somewhere ASAP.

This is the start of my new journaling...

God will set you "aside" until he's prepared you to be used for his divine PURPOSE

- **John the Baptist.....Was set aside.**

  Luke 1: 80..... And the child grew and waxed strong in Spirit and was in the deserts until the day of his shewing unto Israel (to save a nation of people for salvation)

- **Samuel .....Was set aside**

  I Samuel 1: 22 – I will go up until the child be weaned and then I will bring him, that he may appear before the Lord and there abide forever.

  I Samuel 1: 28   I have lent him to the lord: as long as he liveth, he shall be lent to the Lord.

- **Moses .....Was set aside**

  Exodus 2:15 – Moses fled from the face of Pharaoh and dwelt in the land of Midian.

  Exodus 4:19 - and the Lord said unto Moses in Midian, go, return unto Egypt: for all the men are dead which sought thy life (to save a nation of Hebrew)

- **Esther....Was set aside.**

  Esther 2:8 – Ester was brought also unto the king's house to the custody of Hega: Keeper of the women. **Verse 12** – an entire year of preparation,

Verse 15 – Ester obtained favor from all them that looked upon her, **Verse 17** – The king loved her above all women and she was given the Royal crown as queen. **Esther 4:14** –Thou art come to the kingdom for such a time as this? The purpose was to save a nation of her people (Jews.)

- **Joseph ...... Was set aside.**

Genesis Chapter 37:24 Thrown into a pit, a 17 yr. old, a dreamer, loved by his father, but hated by his brothers. **Gen 39:1** Joseph was brought down to Egypt – Potiphar, an officer of Pharaoh, Captain of the guards **Chapter 39:20** thrown into prison **Gen 41:41 (**To save an entire nation from famine)

- **Jonah ...... Was set aside.**

Jonah 1:17- The Lord provided a great fish to swallow Jonah and Jonah was in the belly of the fish for 3 days and 3 nights. (to preach repentance to Nineveh)

 Edith…………. was set aside in prison.

For what purpose does God have for me?

CHAPTER 9
GOD WILL PREVAIL!

June 6, 2017 – What is going on this Monday Morning? All night, I tossed and turned. I just could not even pray myself to sleep. I went to the vendor machines and had gotten a Baby Ruth when another resident came in behind me and bought dill potato chips. I watched another resident sitting at the table waiting to be "drug screened." As the two of them begin speaking, I was out the door heading back to my room. I heard the guard/officer on duty yell – "Hey!" I was not wearing a robe over my T-Shirt and P.J. Bottoms. Not to mention, I was not wearing any under garments under the two pieces. I quickly flew to the bed and got under the covers. Three minutes later, all the lights came on and two officers came into my room demanding that I hand over the food I'd purchased from the vending machine. I quickly hand it to her, a half-eaten Baby Ruth. She then yells, "The next time I call you and you run, you will get a DR, (Disciplinary report) and be heading up 85 North back to prison. "Do you hear me?" I softly replied, "Yes ma'am" and she left. Nowhere in the handbook did I read we could not go to the vending machine after a certain time. I'm shocked that she came looking for me as if I'd robbed a bank. Maybe it was the fact that I ran?

It certainly wasn't that I felt wrong. What I felt was embarrassment for not being properly dressed. I just didn't think I'd see anyone at this wee-hour of the morning. Nevertheless, I'm sure I won't be doing that again. In fact, I've decided to fly completely under the radar. I'm already nicely tucked away from 9:00 am - 6:00 p.m. (nine hours a few days a week) in the GED Lab helping students to get their lesson, preparing them for testing, grading papers and encouraging these ladies to go for a career learning experience. I am a life learner as I love to write, read, study and encourage others to do the same.

Now that I'm in class "Going Deeper with God." I'm being led by the Holy Spirit to just draw back and pray. That is why I say I'm flying under the radar. I don't need to do so much. For example, during inspection this morning, Ms. Lofton asked me "who told you to write a letter to the business office?" I told her that "the officer on duty told me I had to take it up with the business office regarding the money I lost in a vending machine. I called the vending machine place to get them to send a refund to the Business office since they do not allow us to get cash via mail." She questioned me "which officer?" Ms. Smith, Ms. Williams, and Ms. Walker were added to the list – Then I noticed Officer Clark, at the door, I mentioned her as well who did validate that my visitor did lose money in the vending machine.

She eased off and left. I'm curious if I'm over the top doing too much or is this just Satan trying to ruffle my feathers? I'm really seeking to be in the perfect will and waiting to hear from God, Lord Speak! I'm really not sure what's going on. I am reading **Mark - Chapter 1 – 6.** I'm now off to GED class to serve students.

I need to go see my counselor who's been on vacation all last week. I received a notice of my hearing on this past Friday morning from the Georgia Board of Nursing in reference to a sanction or possible revocation of my nursing license. I'm not ready to appear in court to defend my RN license at this time. I have not had time to prep my case or even get an attorney. So, I'm going to have to ask for a continuance. There is no way I'm willing to just walk away from my Nursing license. I don't believe God is going to just let 30 years in good standing go out like this! Not that I need an RN license to work a business, I just can't serve anyone less than 21yrs. Of age, or over 65, or mentally disabled in my business. Well, who else would I service Children? This sentence is just not who I am. I know it, people who know me know it, and God knows. The sentence on paper granted doesn't look good, but that is not a real reflection of me.

I spoke to Chief Jackson about this on Friday. She said I could submit a pass to my counselor Monday so that I could go and handle this situation.

Unfortunately, when I called on Friday and spoke to the judge's assistance, Kevin Westray, he gave me the name of the attorney for the Georgia Board of Nursing. I wasn't able to reach the attorney either. Kevin says, "The judge would like for the parties to meet and try to mediate a resolution before a hearing". But, it's not in my best interest to talk to her without an attorney. She's not for me. That much I know. However, once I believe that I can obtain a continuance, what else the Lord does, it's okay with me. I trust God! Although my flesh is getting worried, I'm not going to even speak it or write it. I am just going to wait and trust God.

When you do what you think you should have done and still get charged, it's a shame. But I must remember God is still in control.

Although I'm angry for someone disrupting my life, and feeling they shouldn't be able to get away with it; I know somehow, some day, God will vindicate, exonerate and handle my enemies. *I dare you to read **Daniel 6:24**.* When God fights for you, there is no worry of retaliation. I am going to rely on the power of prayer. God is able to do exceedingly, abundantly, and above all that we think we can do. In addition to winning, God still gets the glory. That's what blesses my heart!!!

June 7, 2017 – 7:30 p.m., the officers just left the room to count us again. I feel like a little rat getting counted every hour or so. Well, I'm excited that I've "classified" today which means I can wear my own clothes – or donated clothes for now until I can get my own clothes from home when I go on pass prayerfully June 17, 2017. I've submitted or will give my pass request to my counselor to submit to classification next week. I've also got a "special circumstance" pass to go to OSHA court hearing in reference to my RN license. One week from today, if God allows, I plan to speak to an attorney to get advice as I plan to go and speak on my own behalf. Nobody can tell me what I know and feel better than I can. However, I don't know the law and cannot "represent" myself lawfully. Therefore, I had to call Dedric and get legal advice per an administrative attorney. I wanted to say that those "charges" on paper do not signify who I really am.

Yes, I was charged and was subjected to a domino effect plea. However, there were extenuating circumstances that prevailed. I want the opportunity to explain that I'm planning to appeal this case and I'm going to win. I can and will be exonerated and vindicated for this sentence.

Although this sentence has happened and I'm currently serving time for it, it does not warrant my losing my nursing license as an RN. I need to get my court trial deposition papers to see exactly what was said. I know there must be something I can do. I remember Judge

Harris saying something like "no elderly or mentally ill clients in personal care homes". The court didn't say I couldn't work in a hospital, I just remember the Judge saying, (for volunteer or for pay) I cannot work with the mentally ill or elderly. This whole thing still evades me; I will review the records once I'm out.

I believe another lesson I've learned via this M.T.C. transition is to have a broken spirit and contrite heart so that God can use me for his purpose. He's got me on a study of reading about brokenness.

When we are broken to love God more, we see how much our pride separates us from God and how our "own way," the way of the world really doesn't fare so well in the end. **Psalm 51:17** says, **"The sacrifices of God are a broken spirit; a broken and a contrite heart." Oh God thou wilt not despise**. Dwayna Litz says in her book, "Happiness" by God's grace, He makes His own broken and dependent on him." We become broken in a way that makes us better when we live in obedience to the bible, no matter the cost. This is a brokenness that brings glory to God and honor to our lives.

June 8, 2017 - 6:00 a.m. - I am up eating grits and drinking coffee. I am so sleepy. It's Thursday and at 7:00 a.m. I go outside for my "Wellness walk." It's not my best day. 8:00 a.m., I took a nap then prepared for inspection. At 9:00 a.m., inspection took place. No rest for the weary. At 11:00 a.m., Ms. Promise called for me to come to her office to call Attorney Betsey Cohen in reference to the hearing on the 14th. I also called Ozzie to fax a few things and drop off clothes for me to wear to court. It's okay. Gwen versus Ozzie for pick up. Both passes completed just in case Gwen cannot make it. I may not go to court on the 14th. This attorney called back and spoke to the counselor to call me back. When I spoke with her the second time, she's written motions for a continuous as I'm in a transition house with no access to receive all of my records, transcripts or put together my defense or hire counsel. God is so good. She will email and file motion for a joint continuance.

6:00 – 8:00 a.m. - I talked with April Miller until count time. I can call her back again tomorrow at 11:00 a.m. – It's chow time.

9:00 – 10:00 p.m. – Choir rehearsal with Eterica tonight was heavy for me. I could not hold back the tears. I had to open the flood gates of worship to God. Only **He** can stay the hand of the enemy. If God allows a continuous, I will put together a defense to fight for my license. Then I will win. God will prevail. The song we sung in rehearsal tonight was: "Our God is greater

Our God is stronger

God you are higher than any other

Our God is a healer

Awesome is power

Our God, Our God

And if our God is for us

Then who can ever stop us

And if our God is with us

Then what could stand against us

What can stand against us?"

This song - Our God- was written by Chris Tomlin

I know what God can do. I am going to read myself to sleep! All I need to know is what it is he wants? Does he want me to let go or hold on and fight?   Speak Lord, Good Night.

June 9, 2017 - It's Friday today. It is the first day of the rest of my life. **"This is the day the Lord has made; I will rejoice and be glad in it!"** Hallelujah! I've cried my last tear yesterday. I refuse to lose.

Last night, I went to sleep reading, God's Calling   A devotional classic that April Arnold handed to me in Choir rehearsal. When I open the book, the first thing my eyes fell on was "You will conquer." It was April 21 devotion.

Although the actual date in the devotion is June 8th, (and today is the 9th) I'm sure I just opened the devotion to hear what God wanted to say to me today.

I slept so sound someone had to wake me up this morning and by the time I actually got the word of the Lord from this book which read as follows:

("I am with you. My present is a sign of my forgiveness. I uphold you. You will conquer. Do not fear changes. You will never fear changes when I, your Lord change not. Jesus Christ, the same yesterday, today and forever, I am beside you. Steadfastness, unchangingness come to you too, as you dwell with me. Rest in me.

As breathing rightly, from being a matter of careful practice, becomes a habit, unconsciously, yet right preformed, so if you regularly practice this getting back into my presence, when the slightest feeling of unrest disturbs your perfect calm and harmony, so this, too, will become a habit and you will grow to live in that perfect conscience consciousness of my presence and perfect calm and harmony will be yours.")

After reading this devotion, I was able to go outside on my Wellness walk. I talked to the Lord and to my friend, Brunette Nelson. I shared what I read with her.

I attended "Women in Transition" from 10:30 – 12:00 noon. Mama Byrd, 90 years old, taught us the B-Attitudes – Matthew 5: 2-11 (attitudes of gratitude's). I am now being called out by officers. It's 11:00 a.m. to go see my counselor, Mr. Johnson. Praise the Lord! My mom has been approved to come visit. Yeah!!!

The attorney for the Attorney General's Office representative, the Board of Nursing filed for a Joint Motion for a Continuous. She said, "There's no reason for the judge to deny it since we both are making the request. That's good news, but I'm planning on calling her back Monday for sure and my counselor is assigning me with my Golden Pass transportation ensuring that Ozzie will be able to take me even though he's already approved for visitation. He's also on probation. A letter was faxed from his Probation Officer. However, it's the same one sent to E.W.F. back in January. What a crock of B.S. This system is so screwed up. I believe God will prevail on my behalf. I'm just hoping all my items I'm requesting will be approved.

Monday, I'm going out on job search. I had a Brownie and BBQ Pork sandwich with my sisters for lunch. It was good. Thanks April. It's now time to go to work teaching GED student with Ms. Robinson. She also gave me a great Letter of Recommendation that she's already given to my Counselor and Ms. Lofton, Assistant Superintendent. I'm pleased.

3:30 p.m. – Everyone's gone. It's a quiet Friday afternoon. I took a nap, made a few phone calls and went to choir rehearsal.

June 10, 2017 – Mom's approved. However, Ozzie has no car and my sister Gwen and brother James are but arm's reach away. Neither of them has time to bring her, nor drop her off. Its obvious God just doesn't want her to come. I am going back to sleep. It's now count time, then time to study my word and pray. There is a movie called "Inner Peace" showing at the Butler building between 1:30 p.m. and 3:30 p.m. and they had nice Spinach Roll sandwiches with kettle BBQ chips and water.

Yard call did not take place until after 4:00 p.m. count. I chatted with associates until Chow time. I ate 100% of my plate and then got on the phone with Dedric and Ozzie. Neither one had anything worked out regarding transportation. I'm not going to worry at all. There's nothing I can do about it. So, whatever, God is in control! Rest in the Lord.

I'm going to work on my plans for the job search next week and complete my "Golden Pass."

June 13, 2017 – 6:00 a.m. I'm sitting still for the first time today. 7:30 a.m., I sit here in anticipation of the Lord speaking through the women of God, Ms. Charlotte Davis for morning glory prayer. Finally, she is here. 8:00

a.m. and we pray. God told her to anoint all of us to do what he did and greater works. It was good. Then Restoration Network is here to minister from 9:00 – 11:00 a.m. They showed a movie called "Healing Neen," regarding the life of Tonier Cain, which was an awesome video. It inspired me to do more.

Then at 11:00 a.m., Ms. Promise, my Employment Counselor, saw me and told me to come into her office to make calls and complete applications online. This went on until 3:30 p.m. with a thirty- minute lunch break. 4:00 p.m. was count. Then at 4:30 p.m. dinner was served. 6:00 p.m. count, "Women in the Transition" class was not to take place until 6:30 p.m. Then choir rehearsal will begin at 8:30 – 9:45 p.m. I'm exhausted. I'm going to now eat/snack and go to sleep. It's been a long day.

I'm grateful I'm expecting an interview on Monday with a nurse who has her own agency. Prayerfully, if this is what God has for me, Great! I believe God for his perfect will to be done.

June 14, 2017 – It was one week ago that I classified. I've only got two outfits from the clothing closet. I have one pair or white and one pair of black pants, one black and white strip top. I'm so glad. I will be going home this Saturday to get more clothes, personal items and food for my locker, yeah!!!

The clothes don't make me. But it sure feels good to be out of prison clothing. Today, my roomie is classifying. She's so nervous. But I'm sure she's going to make it. Jessica D. was in P.A. school to become a Physician Assistant, when she got hooked on pain pills and heroin. She has now come back to herself. She is still very nervous, but she will be fine. I'm ready to go into the back-class area in GED prep with Ms. Robinson to teach students. This is a rewarding detail. It is certainly better than a cleaning detail, Hallelujah. If this is the Lord's will, I will continue Monday – Friday until my employment begins. I worked until 7:00 p.m., made my bed and did paper work. I then read a little and rested. I'm busy praising and trusting God. He's got me in his hands.

I was awake almost all night. I studied my word and Bible lessons from mail order until 1:30 a.m. I woke up at 3:30 a.m., took a shower and made the bed and dressed. At 4:00 a.m., I washed and dried clothes. At 5:00 a.m., there was a count.

Then I must have finally fallen to sleep because I missed breakfast. The next thing I knew, it was 7:00 a.m. I did my detail in the Laundry room and talked to Nelson, who's here from work today. We will finally have the opportunity to talk Jesus all day.

Vocational Rehabilitation is coming today to see who qualifies for services. So, I'm leaving out now to go to the chow hall for their assessment No inspection for me. Once done, I go back in my room for count. Then I pulled a page out and went to counselor's Gray's office. She had a piece of legal mail for me to sign for - Great! It's a form from the Attorney General's Office from Betsy Cohen. This form had a new court date which was on August 29, 2017. I will prepare and God will go before me. I'm confident God will allow me to keep my Nursing License for his name sake. Although, I will not need them to practice nursing per say, I would like to have the license for C.L.N.C. Certified Legal Nursing Consultant as a precursor to Law school entrance. I'm about to go to lunch now with Nelson.

I enjoyed lunch with my sister in the Lord, Shavonne Giles. I am about to prepare for Bible study. I'm reading and studying and along comes another sister in the Lord Karina Powell joined us. It was great.

Now it's time for me to go to work from 1:00 – 6:00 p.m. with the GED students. Its count time and I fell asleep. **9:30 p.m.** - I was on my feet for another count time. Then I studied the word of God. I'm so grateful and thankful to God for his amazing grace and the power of his word. While I got a letter saying I'm to be in court August 29, 2017 to "defend" my Nursing License, I have no fear, God is my lawyer.

Isaiah 43:1 say "Fear not; for I have redeemed thee. I have called thee by name. Thou art mine. Verse 2 says "When thou pass through the waters, I will be with thee, and though the rivers they shall not over flow thee. When thou walkest through the fire, thou shall not be burned; neither shall the flame kindle upon thee." Now that's a rhema word from the court room of heaven.

God continues to say 41:18 – "Remember, yet not the former things, neither consider the things of old. Verse 19 – "Behold, I will do a new thing, now. It shall spring forth; shall ye not know it? I will even make a way in the wilderness and rivers in the desert." This is God telling me he is going to do the impossible. I believe God is leading me to write my position to present. He will touch the hearts of the opposition and cause the decision to go in my favor. What God wants will prevail. I trust God. I do not have any money for an attorney. But, like the women with "an Issue" after spending all she had and grew worse, God was her healer as he is my defense.

He said in Isaiah 43:26 - "Put me in remembrance. Let us plead together, declare thou, that thou mayest be justified." God is in control. He is the only lawyer I know who's never lost a case!!! "To God be the glory for the thing he has done."

I'm going to continue in his word, trust and obey all the way. Hallelujah.

June 17, 2017 – It's Saturday morning and I am up at 3:00 a.m. I laid in bed until 3:45 a.m. I got up and flat ironed my hair. I couldn't sleep. I was anxious about going home on a pass today. Well, I ate a light breakfast. But I didn't look at the posted approved pass list because I completed my pass with my counselor at Mr. Johnson's desk, as he is the first person who signs off on the pass. I'm sure it's "correct." He called my sister to verify. I was further assured that I was approved because later, Ms. Gray, another counselor called me to her office to give me a letter of legal mail. I asked how I will know if my pass will be approved or not. She said and I quote "We approved them all." No passes were denied. Now I'm really feeling very confident that I'm going home today. About 6:30 a.m., two residents came to my door to tell me that my name is on the list of denied passes. I was shocked. I quickly ran to the window and saw that indeed my name was under this column of denied passes.

It's Saturday morning, no administrative staff or counselors are here. Now what?

I tried to explain to Officer Wiggins that I'm sure it was a mistake and asked her to call whoever is in charge to inquire. Officer Wiggins called somebody and they told her "it was because there was no landline." I was extremely upset because I knew I've had the same landline (770) 943-8277 for eighteen years. (Of course I've changed it now) Quickly, I collected myself and began to speak calmly "I will not be defeated. I will not lose my peace. I will keep my joy regardless whether I go home today or not. I'm at peace. I'm in the center of God's will. I will ask God what am I to learn from this? What's the lesson for me?

Was I too sure of myself? Was he protecting me from something "out there?" Lord, whatever the reason, yea and Amen. You father are in control and always know what's best. I will trust in you is my life's theme."

What I hate about not going is not being able to see all the supporters. Not being able to see Kristy, her new baby, Abigail and her mom, Juanita, one of my favorite clients. They were like family to me. There were many people that were planning to bring items to give me. Paula put a lot of time and energy into cooking the food and making me a cake. I of all people know all so well, you cannot get your time back.

I was not able to go. I spent the day in my word, singing, making melody in my heart to the Lord. My awesome husband Ozzie picked up my mom and they came to see me. They had lunch with me. It wasn't Paula's good Jambalaya, remember, no food can be brought in for visitation. However, we made the best of the vending machines.

After they left at 1:00 p.m., Rev. Ross had a service where I recited the Ten Commandments in numerical order and won a bag of blessings – (Snickers, socks, peppermints, a composition book, a note card and a metered stamped envelope.) It's always exciting to win something!

I'm so sleepy because I've not lain down since 3:45 a.m. this morning. But, I must continue. I finally lay down at 3:30 p.m. after that service and by 6:00 p.m. Another church group was here with powerful praise and worship. I of course got up and attended the service. It's 8:00 p.m. and I lay down again until I hear – "Choir rehearsal." At 8:21 p.m., I'm again in rehearsal until 10:00 p.m. Now I'm going straight to sleep. Phone calls will have to wait. I did send a mass text very early at 9:00 – 10 a.m. to let my supporters know "I would not be home as planned." But I would let them know as soon as I knew when.

The devil got no victory in my not going home. So, he tried something different. I received a call from my son, Travis who tells me he is at Emory Hospital. He said, "He was scheduled to have surgery this week. He is having a colostomy related to Colon cancer. Later, I spoke to the Medical Doctor, Dr. Shaw, who said "they found spots on his liver and lungs. He thinks it may be a spreading of the cancer. He said the Colostomy is necessary to give the colon time to heal."

I know God is a healer. I'm declaring now with fasting and prayer that God will heal his body, deliver his mind and set his soul free. God is able to do exceedingly and abundantly above all we can ask or think.   Travis is unfortunately hard headed and will not do what the doctor said. He's planning to go to church to play the keyboard and then return to the hospital like he's checking in and out of a hotel. He will not listen to me or the MD. Mom and Ozzie went to see him after they left visiting me here at M.T.C. God, my son's in your hands!

June 18, 2017 – It's Sunday and I am sleeping in until the phone rang. It was the doctor and Carolyn Taylor. They discussed a text from Travis. The doctor said "Travis left the hospital without consent and if he comes back with an infection, they will not be able to do the surgery this week." Mom and Ozzie both say they'll talk with him again and speak to the doctors at the hospital regarding Travis.

Now I am on line for inspection. Wow, on a Sunday, oh my God. Oh well, that's the way it is. We usually do not have inspections on Sundays. I'm now up and inspection ready, bed made, dressed and locker straight.

Now that I'm fully awake, I might as well read, write and enjoy a church service on you-tube. I believe I have unlimited data talk and text now.

June 19, 2017 – I got up to shower, dressed and was expecting to have an interview at 1:30 p.m. today with a nurse from a certified nursing assistant school.

I did my hair, put on my makeup and clothes. I had my resume and interview skilled ready. I'm not sure how this position is going to pan out, but, Hallelujah. I called Alice Green to confirm our 1:30 p.m. appointment and she said "I'm glad you called, I have another appointment at 2:00 p.m." we need to reschedule. I asked "if I could come to her facility later this week to see the school and interview there." She said, "Sure, tomorrow, Tuesday at 1:00 p.m." I asked her to call Ms. Promise to make this happen. When I was called to Ms. Promise's office, she called Ms. Green. Ms. Green flipped the script and said "she just talked to me a half an hour ago and told me she could not hire me because of a felony,... what? That was talked about last week. My only issue with her was the W-2 situation.

She said "her administrator told her a felon cannot go to the school as a student let alone work there."

I had sent a text to Ms. Green asking to speak to her to explain my extenuating circumstances. I texted her the number to call Ms. Promise, but she told Ms. Promise "if

I didn't understand our talk one and a half hours ago, she really can't hire me as if I'm slow or something. I felt crushed, but only for a minute. I rejoiced that the devil is mad because I will not yield to his tactics. I don't want anything that is not for me. God has my life in his hand. I don't want to force anything. "Whatever God has for me is for me." He has something better in store. I went on into GED class to teach students, cleaned up my notebook and folders then read the word of God.

6:00 p.m. - I am on the hall phone trying to reach Travis to inform him, "my cell phone is no longer in my possessions and I can't call or text." The officers of C building today took EVERYONES PHONE because the building wasn't cleaned up to their satisfaction. How crazy is that? So, oh well, another trick of the devil. I will not be upset. I've gone fourteen months without a phone. Another week or whatever isn't going to hurt.

6:30 p.m. - I used this evening to fellowship in church/prayer service. Then I had graduation March practice at 8:00 p.m. I then went to choir rehearsal until 10:00 p.m. I'm exhausted. I drank some water and went to bed.

June 20, 2017 – It's Tuesday and I am up at 6:50 a.m. Clothes pressed, makeup on, and hair fixed and ready to start the day. My bed is tight and I'm ready for prayer. 7:00 – 8:00 a.m., prayer with Charlotte Days. It was great day and I had a word from the Lord and the presence of the Lord is here. It was a great service, then I was back in my room resting. Officer Clark came and stood over my bed for a while. I was sleep. She shook my bed and asked, "How can you sleep with someone standing over you?" She asked me "How long have you been in prison?" She was surprised I could sleep so peacefully in prison. I informed her "I can sleep because I knew the prince of peace; I stay in his presence so that he will stay in mine and he makes me very comfortable. God gives his beloved "sweet sleep." She walked away shaking her head.

Now, I'm sitting in "Women's Recovery Network" listening to Mother **Earline Morris** teaching a good word! She's speaking real talk that will help if these women listen attentively and grab hold to this opportunity to take back their lives. She talked about Healing Neen, the movie that we had watched last week.

I went back to my bunk to nap. I read, rested and I'm fasting which took a lot of my physical strength. I have no cell phone to call Dedric, Ozzie or Cynthia. I'm wondering if Travis is having surgery today. I'm wondering how Ozzie is feeling? Is Travis thinking I'm ignoring him? He has no way of knowing I don't have my phone to call him.

June 21, 2017 – Today is a new day and I am going to make it the best day of the rest of this week. God, you are in control and I'm going to be sure to leave everything in your capable hand. It's the day before my interview at a job I don't want. But I believe the other job opportunities will surface if that's the will of God. I've done my due diligence in looking. So now, I'm all in place to wait on God to move. Ms. Promise called to give me the job interview information for the Sweet Tomato restaurant tomorrow at 10:30 a.m. She shared with me a story of a nurse who was here in T.C. before and didn't abide by the rules, and that's one reason she's questioning me. She feels those who don't follow the rules and feel like they want to do their own thing are those who are educated with money and feel empowered. I encouraged her not to judge us all the same.

The graduation rehearsal for "World of Works", **Basics** (**B**ar **A**ssociation **S**upport to **I**mprove **C**orrectional **S**ervices) is not going well. Only 12 – 15 people are here to practice marching in, out of 33-36 that are supposed to graduate.

They changed the song twice and don't want to march. They want to walk with a clap and some of them are just doing something of this nature for the first time. They really do not have a clue. God, grant me with a little more humility and patience please. It takes God's grace to get through this place. They all just want to break the rules. They are smoking in the Bathroom. Now, they are smoking in the Laundry room.

I walked into the Laundry room to clean it, but it was so smoky, I couldn't. The officers walked straight into the laundry room to find the smoking can with cigarettes still smoking out of it and ashes all over the window sill. The officer immediately put us on lock down and of course lots of the females blamed me. I really don't care. I'm not scared of any of these females. Unfortunately, my flesh is alive and well and would almost welcome a fight tonight. I don't smoke and I'm not going to subject myself to second hand smoke. Yes, I told the officer about everyone who was smoking in the Laundry room. I could not clean the room because it was filled with smoke. I did not want an infraction for not doing my detail. That is why I told the officer.

It's Friday and graduation is tonight. Where are the decorations? What an empty day. I'm wearing what I had on twice. They didn't allow Ozzie to bring in what I requested. My counselor finally got the paper work to allow Ozzie to pick me up next weekend June 21, 2017. He's verified the landline as well. Now, I'll just have to submit another Golden Pass again and prayerfully, I'll see my house again sooner than later. I won't be presumptuous. I'll just wait and believe God.

As God would have it, the Commencement speaker at graduation was an attorney who used to be an Administrative Judge. Once graduation was over, I saw her leaving and I told her a little about my upcoming legal hearing. I asked if she'd be willing to look at the case I want to present and give me her opinion. She said "she would." I will have to get her e-mail address from Ms. Michelle Menifee or Mrs. Canton.

I know that was a miracle to have her here and I'm having hope she is willing to look at my situation. I will type and email my documents within a week. Hallelujah.

Saturday, 2:00 p.m. - I'm tired and ready for sleep. But I keep thinking about all I want to get done. Bible study lessons (home study course) needed to be to completed and mailed in, a letter to write to the Judge and Phyllis, a letter to the Georgia Board of Nursing for the upcoming Administrative Hearing to keep my RN license from revocation, completion of my five page Autobiography in order to move to Phase II Movement, clean out and organize my locker, definitely wash clothes (I only have two outfits) and make calls. Without my cell phone, I have to wait in line 15 – 30 minutes at a time. I have to endure all this after a stressful visit with mom, Gwen and Ozzie. Everybody's got a complaint about something. Gwen is being evicted and only has a week to find a place. Ozzie just got a place. Mom is trying to do too much. Travis just had surgery and he's very sick and I'm just too tired to write anymore.

7:00 p.m. – Up for 6:00 p.m. count. Apparently, I went back to sleep and missed dinner. But it's ok. I made a few calls, rested and went back to writing.

8:00 p.m. – My roommate Jessica is back with her stuff and is putting her items away. It looked like half the hall came to be nosey asking to "help her" put it away. She so lame and doesn't understand they are just looking for what they can get out of her, at least some people are. Detail time called – Great, get out of my room!

Sunday - I had breakfast at 6:00 a.m., went back to bed and slept until 10:30 a.m. I showered, shampooed and blow dried my hair, dressed, cleaned, swept and mopped my room. I spoke to Ozzie on the phone and read a magazine. Quiet, all three of my room mates are gone. I am resting in a clean quiet space. Hallelujah!

I went outside to walk, actually studied my bible lessons and a lady walked over to join me. Then another one sat by to listen as I read the study aloud until we were called in for 4:00 p.m. count time. I rested a few minutes and then it was time for chow.

5:30 p.m. – Chow complete. 6:00 p.m. count occurred again and I'm resting. The Pass paper work is complete and ready to turn in.

June 27, 2017 – It's early and I noticed it's unusually quiet. I got into the shower, dressed and curled my hair. The next thing I knew, it was 8:00 a.m. count time. Officer Lewis asked "if I went on the Wellness Walk?" I told her "No." She yelled "Infraction." I said, "I didn't hear it, I was sleep." She went on yelling about how she came to every door telling everyone to go outside for wellness walk! I just didn't say anymore, and I didn't receive an infraction, thank you Lord.

Later, the Employment Manager, Ms. Promise, told me she's waiting for a phone call and will let me know about "my job." All day it was something. My counselor called me to come to his office about my pass. Ms. Promise had denied it because I have "no job." My counselor, Mr. Johnson, had me to come and redo my Golden Pass on gold paper so she wouldn't deny my home pass. Then I had to take this new pass to the nurse to sign off for my eye drops, vitamins and take it back up to his office. Some chick asked if I was waiting for Mr. Johnson. I said yes. She jumped up and said "I'm not waiting; I've heard about you, you're long winded." The devil is a lie! I will not say another word to her and end up saying something I might regret.

Back to GED teaching and I completed both my Autobiography and letter to be e-mailed to the Administrative Hearing Judge Shelton.

June 28, 2017 - 4:00 a.m. – It's count time and I've been moving doing something all day. I got up at 5:00 a.m., dressed, bed rolled up, curled my hair and ready to roll out. I forgot I wasn't supposed to eat and I got blood drawn this am. Oh well, I'll do it tomorrow. Resting and waiting. The next thing I know, its 9:40 a.m. I'm awaking to, "on line for inspection."

Then the officer tells me to report right now to class room 1. There's a lady waiting for me. It was the J.W. Jehovah witness and wasn't it a great bible study. They made some very valid points. Everything they showed me lined up in the bible. That kept me out of inspection and it was 11:30 a.m. when class was over. I got ready for lunch and class.

The rest of the day was nice. I spent time in GED with Ms. Robinson. I left out for Chow at 4:30 p.m. and then again at 5:00 p.m. to wash a load of clothes. Of course, I remained back there as long as I could. Nelson put clothes in the dryer and I stayed lost until 7:00 p.m. I ironed and put away clothes, made my bed and now I'm ready to rest, write and then sleep. It's been another day. Praise the Lord. It's down time from here.

June 29, 2017 – I got up early before any of my roomies. I showered, dressed and made the bed. I'm not curling my hair today. I'm up for breakfast then I remembered I've got to remain up until I'm called for my blood drawn for my chronic care evaluation. Up for inspection, then I went back to sleep until lunch. I am waiting for Ms. Robinson to come for the GED class. I have Bible study to complete; it's a Home Study course I need to mail out.

I was told I will be starting to work next week, July 5, 2017, at the Sweet Tomato. At the first interview, I prayed and believed God that this too will work for my good. No, it's a far stretch from nursing, but, if it's humility he wants, he's got it. I'll start as a dishwasher if you want me too.

I've got God's word that tells me when I acknowledge him and put him first. He's going to provide for my needs. **"Godliness with contentment is great gain."** I brought nothing into this world and it is certain I will carry nothing out. I have food, clothes and with that, I am content. Now Devil, how do you like those apples!

I am still waiting to receive my schedule for work next week. I am waiting here in the GED class with Ms. Robinson. There are no students here today? Only 1-2 dropped in to drop off papers to be graded or worked on the GED pretest which they cannot receive any help. So, it's a great time for me to read.

I did make a folder for the magazine and added the creed I learned at E.W.F.:

> "I commit to having a positive attitude to achieve a successful future.
>
> I commit to making honorable choices for my behavior and actions to exceed limits on expectation.
>
> I commit to reviewing and growing within myself.
>
> I am a sister dedicated to the transformation of mind body and soul."

I see Ms. Promise walking by and looking inside. Ms. Robinson told me that, she was told just today that "Ms. Murry and Ms. Promise complained to her boss that we were too loud." Oh My God, what haters. A few hours later, I'm seeing Assistant Superintendent Lofton walk into the GED room with Ms. Robinson to loudly announce, "Ms. Page has graduated from the area.

She's no longer needed. She's classified and will be working soon so she can go now." I said "ok."

It wasn't fifteen minutes after I'd copied the work Ms. Robinson had just handed me for the students, that the devil reared his ugly head. I knew this was orchestrated by the haters. But, "its ok," I told Ms. Robinson. "I'd not be back after this week anyway because I start my job at the Sweet Tomato next week, Wednesday, July 5.

What was taking so long for me to get a job? I felt that Ms. Promise is purposefully not giving me my Job Schedule so I could not get my cell phone.

However, I later learned that I wasn't hired after I'd given the best interview ever! I was over qualified and the interviewer told her, he didn't need another "manager" he wanted a worker. I realize now I've got to tone it down if I'm going to get a "regular job" after being my own boss for twenty years, it wasn't going to be easy to work for someone else.   I went to eat dinner, rested, read, participated in count, took a shower and got ready for bed. Good night.

Friday – It's the weekend and I'm anticipating going on my first home pass this weekend. I'm not sure how to feel about it because seeing home and not being able to do anything about what I see can be difficult. However, I'm certainly not going to worry. God has it all in his hands. I'm just going to trust that he will allow me to do, see and be just what he wants. I'm sure it's not going to be like I left it. I can't expect anyone to clean my house or take care of it like I would.

I've spoken to Dedric and Paula on a three-way call. He told us he'd put $200 into Paula's account so she could buy the food and give me some money as well. I know he will follow through. Paula's been great trying to call people and let them know I'll be home Sunday for those who can make it. This will be my first-time home since **April 12, 2016.** Oh my God, I'm not sure how I'm going to feel to be going into my home for the first time.

CHAPTER 10
"WHAT GOD HAS FOR YOU IS FOR YOU!"

July 1, 2017 – It's the first day of July – Fireworks! Its official, my name is on the list of approved passes to go home tomorrow, finally. Exactly twenty-one days since I applied for the first pass. Jesus, I know you heard me the first time. But it took the angels twenty-one days to bring me the answer. Whatever God has for me, is for me. <u>Nothing can stop the hand of God.</u> There may be a delay, but "delay doesn't mean denial." God is still on the throne and wrote the end from the beginning so whatever happens is already predestined and fore-ordained. It will happen just like it's planned! So, I've got to start again singing the lyrics to Lauren Daigle song, "I will trust in you."

July 2, 2017 – I got up thinking, I better wash my hair so it will be clean and fresh for Paula or Tony to cut and give me a hair style. Tony is Pastor Deloris William's son. *Styles by Deloris* is the authentic and original, the first African American to have a business in a plaza on Cascade Rd. Pastor Deloris was one of the people who testified at my hearing. Anyway, I flat ironed my hair just a bit so I didn't leave here looking like a scare crow.

I'm wearing a denim skirt and sweater, socks and tennis shoes. I can't wait to get into my own clothes.

When I leave here from the C" building" it's 1:22 p.m., I walked up to the "A building" and see my husband and mom in the car waiting. I go into the "A building" to sign out and they tell me to have a seat. I have to leave at exactly 1:30 p.m. At 1:28 p.m., they give a copy of my pass and say, "Have a good time."

I looked at my "golden pass" paper of the things I was planning and had requested to bring back to M.T.C. I saw that there were so many no's next to the things I'd requested. I was told by one officer that the pass is "golden" and you could request pretty much anything that of course wasn't contraband. However, so much of what I'd requested, has a big fat **no!** written next to it. But of course, the officers said, "we don't have anything to do with anything. That's what the committee wrote, that's what you can bring or not bring back. Bye."

Riding in my Avalon for the first time since April 12, 2016, I noticed the right door mirror was gone. There was a scratch down the right door and it was dirty. I became a little frustrated. Quickly, I must readjust my thought process.

It's only six hours before I must be back here. So, I'm telling myself, there's nothing you can do about anything. So, let it go. Focus on the entire positive of going home and what I'm about to experience. Mom is in the back seat. I quickly get over to her for a hug. Ozzie is in the driver's seat, I opened the door; I hugged him, and we were off. A little scarred of his driving, but in my mind, I rebuked accidents and held on.

Straight to the house, I noticed my trees are all over grown. I noticed the lake was high crossing the driveway. A piece of the driveway was totally washed away. My yard is a mess. But the house is still standing and I'm grateful for that. It's not as clean as I'd like. However, I thank God things are as well as they are. I can't be embarrassed about the front porch or the grass because nobody is going to treat your home as you would. Let it go!

Ozzie goes to Red Lobster to pick me up a good Seafood meal. It was good. But I would have enjoyed the wings from Publix's better. I won't complain. He spent his last $32 to buy that for me and I'm thankful. Based on the list of items I requested, Ozzie has almost 99% of what I asked for to be taken back with me to M.T.C. here at the house.

Visitors are coming soon to see me for the first time since my incarceration in 2012. My dog King, my baby that was given to me by Travis (half Maltese and half Shiatzu mixed), greets me with all his love. I can't put him down for at least a half an hour. I love my dog. He loves me back, his bark; a whimper, tells me he missed me.

Then the guest began to arrive. Pat Bowen is the first to arrive, my dear friend. Charlotte, Mr. Grant's sister, arrived and we talked with him. I tried not to talk business and stuff because it's hard trying to conduct business from M.T.C. I can talk, but I'm technically still locked up. There's very little I can do. Then came Paula, Pastor Deloris and her son, Tony, who gave me a sharp haircut. Angela Glaude-Hosch, Carolyn Taylor, my brother James and his three girls arrived. Then others arrived, Gwen, Sharon Beaner and her mom Ms. Dickson. Everyone brought me something to take back to M.T.C. Thank you, Jesus for supportive friends and family. I wish Cynthia and Dedric could have been here, I enjoyed the fellowship of friends so very much. Tony gave me a super haircut and Paula Cook flat ironed and styled it, and man do I look fabulous!

It's time to return. Where did the time go? I packed up my goods, hugged necks and headed back to M.T.C.

I'm remembering all that I've done and what I'm going to do next. I'm absolutely going to study law to make sure I don't go back inside again. I pray God has done all he needs to do with me on the inside and let me work from home on the outside, to help those still incarcerated.

Somewhere in my journaling, I remember telling God, "I'll go." Lord, if you need somebody send me, I'll go. Well, this may have been the test to see if I really meant what I said because, here I am sitting in a half-way house after a prison sentence? God spoke to me and said: <u>A flashlight serves no purpose in broad day light</u>. It is in the darkest place where a light is needed. That's revelation, now I understand.

I'm back from my home pass and it was good, not great, but good. I'm back here at M.T.C. putting away many things. I enjoyed fellowship with my roommates, until the lights were turned out early, due to somebody smoking in the bathroom. This place with its mass punishment isn't right. That's a system problem. They need to come up with a better way of catching and disciplining those who are wrong rather than taking everyone's phone and privileges. All is well. It is well! I'm going to bed now by default.

July 3, 2017 – It's a M.T.C. holiday celebration for us residents. We're supposed to have what they call "Fun day." We will have games, food, fun, music, dancing, a talent show, and contest with all the holiday goods to go with it. Sargent Bynum was on duty and waking everyone up by 7:00 a.m.

I got up, cleaned up, and then went outside walking for an hour. Then, as soon as I get to sleep around 10:00

a.m., they're calling us outside again to play games. I'm outside, but 90% of everyone is sitting around looking. There are a few people participating, but it's the same people playing these games.

Some people are playing spades inside. Some cheated and snuck back to their bed and the watermelon is being passed out.

Now, its talent show time. I helped set up chairs and the talents were amazing. There was singing, dancing, rapping and of course, a 19 – year old rapper won. That's the age we're living in. I don't get it. Oh well, that's the nature of this place. Sinners, Sodom and Gomorrah. I'm getting out and not going back, except to help when I'm led to do so...

July 4, 2017 – I'm awake. I had potatoes, eggs, grits, a banana, bread and coffee for breakfast. I read my bible and rested until Ozzie came to visit. He's here! But, not well groomed. I think he's depressed. He didn't stay very long. We talked superficially but, he did say he was going to see Travis and find out how he's doing. Outside it's warm and humid, but there is a breeze.

I'm back inside now and I am going to sleep. My Bunkie wakes me up. It's 4:00 p.m. Count time and I am going back to sleep. I am not hungry. I am taking my hamburger and hot dog back to my room to eat later. I'm just not able to eat. I called Ozzie and he told me how bad the news is with Travis. I'm tearful, but hopeful. Everybody I called eleven different people, and no answer from anyone. God must just want me to call on him.

"I will bless the Lord at all times." His praise shall continually be in my mouth. My destiny doesn't have to look like my history. The word of God directs my steps period! God is in control – Regardless.

I know I can and will have what I say. The entire world was created, conditioned and controlled by words.

Words start with my thoughts. I will think on those things that are honest, true, and lovely and of a good report, thoughts, and words will reproduce after themselves.

Joshua 1:8 – Mediate on it!

This book of the law, shall not depart out of thy mouth, but thou shall meditate on it day and night, that thou mayest observe to do according to all that is written there in, for then thou shall make thy way prosperous and thou shall have good success.   THIS IS MY FAVORITE SCRIPTURE IN THE ENTIRE BIBLE.   I've lived and loved this one for over 40 years.

Invent, create, build, and network. This will fuel my daily words. **Thoughts –become words, and words become - action, actions become – habits, habits create change –**

and change is what brings you to your destiny. (Another WOF saying I live by)

 Command your morning by speaking what you want.

Proverbs 18:21 says Death and Life are in the power of your tongue: and they that love it shall eat the fruit thereof. Choose what you want, Edith!

Job 22:28 – Thou shall also decree a thing and it shall be established unto thee: Speak authority over your life!

July 5, 2017 – I got up, showered, got dressed and was ready to go to work early. No breakfast for me as I'm looking forward to eating at Sweet Tomato Restaurant Ms. Promise finally called me. I completed the application and went back to the room and waited.

I needed to see Counselor Johnson to plan to go see Travis. Ms. Promise happened to come to the hallway during inspection time to discuss someone from Nancy's Pizza will be coming to host a Job Fair tomorrow here in the lobby at 2:00 p.m. She said, all in need of work, to prepare hair and make up for an interview." I didn't plan to participate because I'm going to start today at Sweet Tomato, or at least I thought so.

I went to the Sweet Tomato. However, I wasn't hired. That's a second rejection. That's something I'm not used to, being told, no? Is that the lesson I 'm supposed to learn here? I think I "over sold" myself. A second interview, a second person, same sweet tomatoes and no hire....

Friday – I finally think I'm going to see Travis at the hospital. Cynthia faxed the birth certificate. Ozzie faxed our marriage license. I'm going up to the top "A building" to meet with Chief Jackson at 8:30 a.m. I am met with all kind of drama. She accused me of Travis being my step son and falsifying documents. She also said, "I was lying and playing games." Chief said, "I received two faxes from two difference social worker." Everything that could go wrong did. Since I'm a nurse of thirty years, she accuses me of probably knowing people at the hospital and they got their wires crossed. Apparently, two different people sent two different faxes? One from the nurse I spoke to on the unit and one from the Hospice social worker where my son was being transferred to. I had nothing to do with what was on it. However, it's still the same message. MY SON WAS DYING! Why do I have to explain myself, AGAIN!

But the devil is still a liar. I'm going to see my son. They told me, "no." I leave "A building" and go back to "C building" to go to Mental Health. I requested to see Ms. Stucky, the counselor, who helped me. Finally, she got security to take me for an hour or so. I saw Travis. He cries, I cry and somehow, we sing and praise God together.

I'm spending the rest of my time neatly writing Travis. No more journaling tonight for me. I'm going into prayer and writing to my son.

July 8, 2017 – 2:00 p.m. – I just finished visitation with mom and Ozzie here at M.T.C. They're going to see Travis, now. I sent a letter to him that I wrote last night called, _A Mothers Love_. I let Travis know, I didn't get it all right. I've asked for his forgiveness. I shared my heart and I prayed for God's peace over his life and opened him up for pure forgiveness and restoration for our relationship. Never did I ever imagine Travis, who loved the Lord, having an illness/disease that could take him. It just never resonated in my mind. I'm praying, trusting and believing God to restore and mend our hearts together. I want pure reconciliation and the love of God to run deep knitting our hearts together in love based on the word of God. God is still a healer and a deliverer. I trust him to do what he does best, keep his word!

July 9, 2017 – 6:00 p.m. - Bless you Lord! Paula came to visit me here at M.T.C. This morning, she was a welcomed face. Joy, love and peace in the Holy Ghost. We prayed and shared. Yesterday was wonderful but today's church service was not what I'm used to. Nevertheless, the lady tried hard. They did pray in the end. The prayer touched my heart and I cried so hard when she called Travis name. I sat and cried.

They dismissed and came over to lay hands and prayed for me further. One lady said, "Don't cry because that allows doubt to set it." Once they all left, I was able to cry out to the Lord. I cleaned up my face and left out. This evening will be praise and worship filled to my Father God Jehovah!

July 10, 2017 – I'm awake early with the lights on. My prayer and thoughts are heavily on my son. I showered, groomed and dressed, made the bed, got locker inspection ready and placed the laundry out the door. No breakfast is needed this morning. I have no appetite. I've written a letter to Ms. Promise asking to be sent out to work today. My prayer is to be where God would have me to go. Today Jesus, please today.

I've seen Ms. Promise and let her know I put a note into her box and I am willing to work anywhere. She ignores me. I'm waiting to be called to her office. It's now 5:00 p.m. and I see her walking out into the Lobby with her purse and bag. So, I say, rhetorically, "I see you are leaving for the day?" She responds, "No, I'm just carrying my purse, bag and lunch bag, very sarcastically. She's so "bitter," Jesus take the wheel! Maybe tomorrow will be better.

July 11, 2017 – I'm hopeful and prayerful that this day will be better. Sergeant Bynum is yelling early "Wellness walk." I'm up and ready, although its prayer time this a.m. at 7:30 a.m. If Ms. Charlotte is on time, I'll walk until she gets here. I am up walking and talking with Brittany Moore. She tells me there is an opening at McDonalds. She worked there six months and is now a manager. Now it's on, I am planning to tell Ms. Promise to send me to Mickey D's.

My prayer with Charlotte Davis was awesome and the Women of Recovery Network is directly behind them. They prayed with me and for Travis as well. I truly believe God will hear and honor my Hezekiah prayer on the wall! Finally, Ms. Promise called me and gave me an interview slip for an upscale Italian restaurant. I will go to it tomorrow. I'm hopeful for a position as a hostess. I am so excited! Midtown or Buckhead area is where I'm told House Wives of Atlanta eat/film at for their show.

I met with "Women in Transition" at 6:30 p.m. Stacy and her mom were assigned to me. I will be their mentee and I'm looking forward to it. Also, she prayed for Travis in our closing prayer.

July 12, 2017 – It's Job day! Hallelujah!

"Father God, in the name of Jesus, I thank you in advance for what you are doing in this day that you have made. I will rejoice and be glad in it, Amen."

Its count and inspection going on at the same time, that's not the usual. The officers are up yelling at 5:00

a.m. for people to get up and do their details. Today is T and I day. This is the day we receive money for Transportation and Incidentals. I'm waiting to be called for our hall to go pick up T and I.

I get up to shower, dressed and I ironed clothes for my interview. I'm excited to be going out today. Italian food, yum. I'm so looking forward to this wonderful day! I see Ms. Kennedy the Warden from Alto, walking with the inspection team Assistant Superintendent Ms. Lofton and Chief Jackson.

The Warden comes to my room, I smile. We talked and shared my expected experience. She responded, "You've got the disposition for the job as hostess." I told Ms. Lofton, "I'm not coming back without a job!"

11:00 a.m. – 11:30 a.m. I have a doctor's appointment. All is well. Finally, 12:30 p.m., it's time to go. I took my lunch and I left. I am so excited. I am outside in the beautiful sunshine.

I had an easy bus and train ride. However, I had to do a 2-3 block walk that made me sweat my makeup. I finally arrived at this exclusive-midtown restaurant with nice décor. As soon as I walked inside hot and sweaty, the manager is sitting at the door/corner bar stool. So, I had no opportunity to go to the restroom and collect myself. I immediately tell him" I'm Edith. I'm here to meet with Mr. Stephan's." He replies, "I am Mr. Stephan and it was over. I told him I'm from M.T.C. sent by Ms. Promise for an interview. I think he just "sized me up with all the gray hair." He said, "I don't have any positions open, but let me get you an application." I proceeded to complete the application as neatly and completely as possible. I all but begged for any position. He didn't even interview me. He just looked over the application and didn't ask any questions and I didn't offer any explanations. After pleading for any position, I humbly asked him to call Ms. Promise because I'm expected to come back with a job.

His assistant came over and she introduced herself to me. She seemed empathetic. She began scrolling through her phone looking for nearby places that were looking for a hostess. She said, "The Twelve Seasons and Renaissance Hotel has restaurants just around the corner. They have hostess positions and I could go apply there." But, of course, I have to go back to M.T.C. and go through Ms. Promise.

I return extremely disappointed more so because I could not get my phone to talk to my son until I get a job and I can't get a pass to see him because I don't have a job. That's what's really heart breaking.

Anyway, I made my bed and laid down waiting for Ms. Promise to call me. I finally sat in the Day Room looking out for Ms. Promise 7:30 p.m., I'm sure she's gone home by now. Oh well...

I used the hall phone to call and spoke with Travis, Cynthia, Paula and Ozzie. I'm going to read myself to sleep. Thank you, Lord, it's as well as it is. I will not complain. I'm only asking for grace, mercy and peace for me and Travis on this journey. Good night.

July 13, 2017 – It's 4:00 a.m. and I am wide awake. I've gone to the bathroom, bathed, groomed and dressed. I have journaled, read and my mind keep taking me where I don't want to go. Please Jesus, mercy. I didn't eat because I did not have an appetite. I had coffee and my blood pressure pills. I'm getting into my word!

I spent time in my word, and journaling in my new hard bound journal. Let your request be known into God. This journal was given to me by Angela Glaude - Hosch. I've asked God to give me my son back because there's so many stories in the bible where God restored, healed and rose from the dead, sons that were given back to their mothers. Based on the word of God, a nobleman's son healed from the point of death, a widow- her only son was dead and you had compassion for her and raised the young man and he sat up and began to speak, YOU gave him back to his mother and YOU were glorified throughout all the region (**Luke 7: 12-17)** The Shunamite woman didn't ask for a son but YOU gave him to her, allowed him to die, and used your servant to raise him back to life. (**II Kings 4:28-37**) Jairus petitioned you to come to his house to heal his only daughter and YOU raised her up to life (**Luke 8: 41-42 and 50-56**) YOU spared Isaac Abraham's son**,** YOU provided a ram in the bush **(Genesis 22: 12-13)** Lord, you have a ram…. Tears flow as I begin to pray…

Father God Jehovah, My one and only true and living God, God of the universe, creator of heaven and earth. I come boldly to the throne of grace to receive mercy and find help in my time of need. You have only one begotten son and I know it bruised you to give him up, but you being all powerful, raised him from the dead. Please let me remind you of your word; you said in Isaiah 41:21 Produce your cause, saith the Lord, bring forth your strong reasons saith the King of Jacob, God; you are not a man that you should lie nor the son of man that you should repent, so if you said it, you must make it good. You said in Isaiah 55:11 that your word cannot return unto you void so God, I have reminded you of many of the son's you gave back to their mothers, please give mine back to me. You are no respecter of persons so if you've done it before, you can do it again, you're the same God yesterday, today and forever and you change not! You healed all manner of sickness and disease, cancer is not too hard for you. I'm humbly asking you to give me my son back, add years to his life like you did for Hezekiah, and raise him up as a testimony for your glory! Father, your word is sure; not one word of all your good promises have failed…. (I feel like I can hardly breathe here)…. In the name of Jesus, I command my emotions to be still and rest and trust as your word works, in the mighty, matchless name of your son Jesus the Christ…. AMEN!!   I've made my request known.

Later, I go into the day room and studied with Ashley who goes by the name Goldie. She is a 30 - year old young woman who's studied the word for years, she only needs to be refreshed and restored to trust God and speak his word. We studied together until they call mandatory Yard call. I'm waiting to sign out, but Ms. Promise calls me into her office, Hallelujah.

OK, I'm quiet, waiting and allowing her to do all the talking. She informs me of a position at a Hotel where there is a housekeeping job. "Cool" I'll take it." You will work alone cleaning rooms occupied and unoccupied. "I can do it, no problem."

This job is located near Cumberland which is close to my home, that way I can keep it for a while once I'm out of M.T.C.

I'll leave at 5:30 a.m. and stay out all day! I'm outside now. Chief will finally give me my phone. I'm so ready. I get back inside and call Paula and Ozzie to tell them about my job and who but Ms. Promise sees me on the hall phone. She walks over to tell me, "it's not 4:30 p.m. and you're not supposed to be on the phone until after 4:30 p.m." I say "OK." Then she says, "You can forget about your next pass, for being on the phone, and not following the rules. These rules apply to you too, Ms. Page. "You got that." I say, yes ma'am, and go to my room. She has a way of making you feel like a child.

I'm so over this place. It's ok, because I am going to get what I need, and do what I need to do. I'm just going back under the radar and try my best to work as much as possible. I'm so over Ms. Promise. Its Chow call and I had no appetite.

I'm almost ready for bed. It's 8:00 p.m. Come on 9:00 p.m. count. I'm sleepy.

Friday – It's 5:30 a.m. and I've got to catch the bus at 5:57 a.m. I took a quick shower, got dressed, hair done and out the door.

Wow, fifteen people getting on the bus. It was a long ride. When we get to five points downtown Atlanta, everybody scattered, oh my God. I thought those who leave together, come back together. Where's everyone going? Wow, well technically, we are all still here at five points, so I guess it's not "really deviating." Lord forgive me because Five Points is for transportation, not for eating at underground and I know that. My mind says; make no provisions for the flesh. It would be my luck someone sees me. Just because all the other people scatter doesn't mean I have to. If I do that, then it will make it easier to break the rules in other areas I'm thinking to myself. I am going to write a Letter of Apology to Ms. Promises for breaking the rules.

Oh no, not another job fiasco. Upon getting off the bus, I can see across the street the hotel, there appears to be a fire at this job site when we arrive. All the hotel guests are outside. A fire truck is pulling up into the parking lot.

After an hour outside, we wait inside another hour. Then we find out the person to interview us in not even there today. We were told to "come back on Sunday" at 8:00 a.m. to meet this person who's to interview and do our paperwork and video training.

July 15, 2017 – Hallelujah, another day the Lord has made**, "I will rejoice and be glad in it!"** I am studying the book of Psalms this morning with Shavonne Giles. We are having Coffee, Bagels with Cream cheese until count time.

After count, I read and it is finally time for visitation. I'm expecting Dedric today. We have a lot to catch up on. Visitation is from 9:00 - 1:00 a.m. today. I ate two sandwiches, three bags of chips, a honey bun and a sprite. I am full. It's nap time. I attended church service, praised and worshiped, then went to sleep.

It's now chow time. I got a little more rest then phoned a few of my friends and family. Thank you, Jesus, all is well. I then read God's word and spent time with him.

I had an excellent day. I now must get ready for work tomorrow. I'm excited to be getting out!

July 18, 2017 – My last journal entry was Saturday. Sunday was awfully busy and work transportation was a pain. Monday wasn't a whole lot better. I don't even care to journal the experience.

Work is hard at the hotel. Bending and making beds is no joke. I'm not use to this hard labor, but I'm going to get it done. I can do whatever I must do for ninety days. After ninety days is when you can go back into job search for something you want.

I spoke with Travis on the phone on Saturday morning and told him I was not permitted to get a pass until Thursday, July 27. and I could be there by 11:00 a.m. Late this same evening, I received a call that my son would not make it through the night. I begged to be able to go to the hospital to be by his side. The officers on duty wanted to take me, but had to get it Okayed by Chief. I informed Chief that the doctor called asking me to come, because his heart rate was 165 temp 104.4 and they don't think he's going to live through the night. Chief replied, "I don't care if God himself called, you ain't going nowhere tonight". I was painfully numb.

On July 27, as I was preparing to leave, the officers could not locate my pass. By the time the officers located the pass, I did not arrive at the hospital until

<u>11:30 a.m</u>. I was met at his hospital door by his father and my family when they informed me that <u>he had passed at exactly at 11:00 a.m.</u> I just fell across his deceased body and cried.   After holding him for a while, my body slid to the floor and on my knees, I just worshipped God.

August 12, 2017 – 4:56 p.m., I have not journaled here in almost one month. **July 19th – August 11th**… No entries in my journal,   I had been writing to God in my Black Journal that says "Let Your Request Be Made unto God." That was given to me a few weeks ago by Angela Glaude–Hosch; *A Heavenly Anointed Vessel who Evangelized Nationwide*, I met her April 20, 2013 at Mt. Sinai women's conference.   This woman spiritually "saved my life".   Anyway; the only thing I've been writing in this journal is prayers, request and scriptures for God to spare my son. But now that he's gone which took place on *July 27, 2017*, I have to trust and just keep it going. I am not sure what else I'm going to write in this beautiful Journal.   Maybe, I'll pick up here writing about my son's daughter's life.   My one and only granddaughter, Ka'Laybria Meshell Turner.

This August 12, 2017 makes two days shy of a month that I began working at the hotel, July 14, 2017. I'm cleaning rooms and making beds for hotel guest, occupied and unoccupied. I'm always seemingly, the first one to get started and the last one to leave. But, it's okay. I know I do a great job because I work as unto the Lord!

I can't journal much day or night like I use to. I've been spending more time in prayer talking to God and hearing what he has to say rather than writing and telling him what I want to say. **God's purpose is so much greater than my plans.** So, when my plans get thrown, I don't sweat it anymore. I see and recognize the enemy and he will not win! I'm keeping my peace and my joy! Devil you lose again!!!

It's been a week since I funeralized my son. It's alright Lord, I still love you and I'll forever praise your name. I cry and sing while I work, the only "alone time" I have.

August 27, 2017 – It's been exactly thirty days ago today that I lost my only son, Travis, to Colon Cancer. It's difficult to say, he's gone. I believed he's with the Lord and that gives me some comfort. But a Mother's love never dies. I'm still wearing one of his Dreadlocks around my wrist. I think about him every single day.

I cry, I pray and I sing. I still praise God. But yet, it still hurts. I'm keeping busy working and focusing on something else to keep my eyes dry.

August 29, 2017– I'm not writing much anymore because Carpel Tunnel has returned. My hands hurt to write and my fingers tingle. The tips are swollen and burgundy/purplish like my circulation is sluggish. I've put in a request to my counselor to see a medical doctor for an assessment a week ago. She has not replied.

I attended the OSAH Office of Administrative Hearing today in reference to my Nursing License. I pray Judge Kristen rules in my favor.

September 5, 2017 – I try hard not to think about Travis. I need a place and space to grieve properly, if that makes any sense. Living in a small room with three other females is not exactly conducive for me to neither express nor handle how I am truly feeling. It's been exactly thirty-days ago since we funeralized him.

My fingers are painfully on fire. So, I won't write much now. But there's plenty to say. I'm still angry about his father not attending his own son's funeral. He sent flowers. However, this was your only son. How could you not pay your last respects? I'm grateful his father spent the last days of his life by his side. He took a few pictures showing the few days they spent together. This was when Travis was up and around, but NOTHING can replace you not attending his final day on earth.

Tony, I've called him all his life, Thomas Anthony McClendon; Travis's father, texted me asking how I'm doing? I didn't even reply. In fact, I blocked him from calling or texting me. I'm really hurting inside. God will allow me to forgive him in time.

Our connection, our son Travis, is gone and Tony you are history! At least while I'm grieving. Lord, help me to forgive him... **October 16, 2017 –** Today marks 90 days of employment at the Hyatt hotel as a housekeeper, a very humbling experience, but I've got the lesson now and I'm ready to move on to my new blessing. Lord, you are the only one who knows what's really going on and why. I wish you'd let me in on it, but I trust you as you know what's best for me. This morning I was held in by officer Flemings so I could talk to someone. When I came in last night, she told me she could "feel my fullness" and I needed to talk to somebody. I started to cry because she was right; I need to get it out, I'm so ready to leave this place. I came in late from the job because I fell asleep on the bus and missed my stop. Being it was a Sunday it took longer for another train and bus to get me back to MTC. This morning I was called to the bubble to receive a DR. I'm being punished because I was exhausted, people here do all kinds of stuff and don't get into trouble... I had to talk to my counselor, the mental health counselor and the supertendent Ms. Osborn who thought I might be a "flight risk" as I am overwhelmed with this place. Where am I going to run to? Yes, I'm tired and angry but I'm not trying to run away... and have 5 to 10 years added to my sentence, that's ridiculous. I wrote my position statement and the DR was not given, thank you Jesus.

CHAPTER 11

TRUST IN YOU!

I don't know what's next. What I do know is that I will trust in you, Lord. That reminds me of a song written by Lauren Daigle called, "Trust in You." So many of her songs speaks to seeking God. **TRUST IN YOU means to let go of every single dream and lay them down at the feet of Jesus. We may wonder and wander in our minds but what we see doesn't change what God sees for our future. I'm not interested in trying to do anything on my own, I may start out strong in my flesh but I will get weary and give up, but if God is leading and guiding as he promised in Psalms 32:8 I can trust and wait for him. I don't even need to think about how to make it work when I've got a guide, all I have to do is sit back and ride and leave the driving to God.**

I trust God to lead, guide, strengthen, and comfort through the journey. God already knows what tomorrow will bring, there's nothing I can go through that he's not already seen. The bible says his ways are higher than my ways and he's already written the end from the beginning, the fight is fixed, I win!

So, why do we fret and sometimes worry? Because we don't know what the word says about us, we don't trust in the songs we sing about, we don't believe what God has told us in the light when we come into a dark place.

But this has shown me that I can trust God though anything. For all my haters and those who thought they were going to destroy me, let me serve notice on you that the God that I serve is greater. You would do better to tie a millstone on your own neck and throw yourself into the depths of the sea than to mess with me.

God is my steady hand a rock and a firm foundation on which I stand. I shall not be moved!

So how does it all end? Well it's not over yet. Here's what's going on as I write the end of this book.

I'm home, as of **July 2, 2018**, but still haven't totally adjusted if you can understand that. There is still so much to be done. Swamp, trees, driveway, landscaping... I still need time to properly grieve the loss of my only child.

Bishop Bronner did write me back with a card "from the desk of Dale C. Bronner" in his own handwriting with such powerful, prophetic, and encouraging words. My Registered Nursing Licensed was revoked here in Georgia, and it's ok, yep... it really is OKAY.

A month later or so, I voluntarily surrendered my California RN license as well. This was a domino effect where the enveloped was pushed to make sure I didn't make any good money as an RN. I believe Cobb County pushed it, nevertheless... What I do know, is that God has bigger and better plans than I had.

I'm still working at the hotel. However, I am no longer in housekeeping. I was promoted to work at the front desk after six months of being a housekeeper. Now, I check our guest in and out of the 3 star hotel answering phones and assisting wherever I'm needed. In addition, God opened a door while I was in the transition center where I began attending a private college to obtain a Bachelor of Science in Legal studies. I currently have 20 credit hours completed with a 4.0 GPA, with only three more semesters to complete. I will then bridge into Law School.

I was released from the Transitional Center just three months ago. I had planned to take my first week and just relax on a beach, take the opportunity to just breath, body scrub all the "prison" scales off me with a wonderful spa body scrub, enjoy a massage, facial, manicure, pedicure and colonic. (This I missed doing on a regular basis like I used to). I just wanted to get refreshed from the inside out and of course go to church.

Well, the reality of that was my first day home was "paralyses by analysis." I could not do anything but look around at all that needed to be done. Trees had terribly cracked my driveway, water from the swamp lake had ruined another section of my driveway and several tree limbs needed to be cut down. My car needed some major repairs and parts replaced.

My house and carpets needed to be cleaned and I just thought about all that at one time, and couldn't do anything….Paralysis by analysis…

Well, after a few days of fasting and nightly soaking in my Jacuzzi tub, sleeping in my wonderful temper-pedic bed and praying for some direction, God answered prayer. I woke up one morning to find Greystone Power Company had sent a bucket truck in front of my house and all the way down my driveway (600 feet) to cut limbs that were on *their* power lines. I heard limbs being cut and saw them taken away at no cost to me. The next day I met someone who not only provided beautiful lawn care, but was able to stabilize my driveway at a very affordable cost.   In addition to that, my car was given a brand new, not rebuilt; but a brand-new engine and transmission, new rotors and brakes front and back, tire rods and whatever else needed to be fixed all for a miraculous price of a little more than $5,000. It runs and feels like a brand-new car, without the car note and the high insurance premium that comes with a new car. All my nice clothes are still here (thank you mama Beeks) and minimal materially has been lost; However, physically and emotionally, I've lost my son and time.

Only God could allow me to go through the floods and not allow the water to overtake me, only God could take me through the fire and not allow me to come out burned and not even smelling like smoke; **Isaiah 43:2.**

God is still in control and I will never stop saying it. What was meant for my destruction has and will continue to turn out for my good. *Throw me to the wolves and I will come out leading the pack.*

Although Daniel was set up **(Daniel 6:11-16),** Daniel came out of the Lion's Den, unharmed, his haters were dealt with, and everyone was made to honor the God of Daniel. **(Daniel 6:23 - 26)** Joseph came out of prison second in command to Pharaoh, **(Genesis 41:40).** Paul and Silas, Peter, James, John, and according to my research; so many men in the bible who really did anything for God, went to prison. No, I'm not saying that prison is necessary for God's glory, but for those of us he has allowed to take this path, makes me feel better now about knowing that I was not out of fellowship nor out of the will of God, "because" I went to prison.

Nelson Mandala came out of prison and became the President of South Africa and Edith is now out and God has great plans for my future that will glorify him and make my natural and ministry family proud. This plan I will not give away, but all I can say is look out! GOD will be magnified and glorified; and the enemy will be horrified.

I will remain faithful to the task and God of course is always faithful to his word! My brokenness is becoming a work of art in the Masters' hand. He is the potter, I am the clay being made, shaped and molded to his likeness.

There are too many scriptures that assure me of his faithful covenant. I will list just a few here for you to etch in your memory. If you can read, speak and hold these scriptures near and dear to your heart, I promise you, it will make a difference in your life.

1. Proverbs 30:5

EVERY WORD OF GOD IS PURE: HE is a shield unto them that put their trust in him.

2. Psalm111.7

The works of his hands are verity and Judgement; *ALL his commandments are sure.*

3. Ezekiel 12:25 For I am the Lord; I will speak, and the word that I speak *SHALL COME TO PASS;…*

4. Luke 21:33

Heaven and earth shall pass away,; but my words shall not pass away.

As long as you believe God's word, trust and obey when he speaks, there is no way you can lose!

5. <u>Numbers 23:19</u> - God is not a man that he should lie; neither the son of man that he should repent: hath he said, and shall he not do it? Or hath he spoken, and shall he not make it good?

6. <u>Deuteronomy 7:9</u> - *KNOW* therefore that the Lord thy God, he is God, the faithful God, which keepeth covenant and mercy with them that love him and keep his commandments to a thousand generations.

7. <u>Isaiah 55:11</u> So shall my word be that goeth forth out of my mouth; it shall not return unto me void, but it shall accomplish that which I please, and it SHALL prosper in the thing whereto I sent it.

8. <u>II Corth 1:20</u> for ALL the promises of God are Yea and in him AMEN...

9. <u>Hebrews 6:18</u> It is IMPOSSIBLE FOR GOD TO LIE..

10. <u>Roman 8:28</u> - And we know that all things work together for good to them that love God, to them who are the called according to his purpose.

CHAPTER 12
LESSONS LEARNED

While in prison, I learned a lot of lessons I would like to share with you!

- I was in prison, but prison was not in me!

- I was locked up, but not locked in mentally.

- I used my God given talents to please God and man.

- **Your bible is your weapon of freedom while God work's his plan!**

- What you do today, determines your tomorrow!

- You can find peace in the middle of a storm, you don't have to borrow!

- Trust God and lean on him for understanding!

- Learn all you can and take what you've learned with you, should be the plan!

- Stay out of trouble, associate with people who have the same values as you!

- Teach and share your knowledge with others until you are through

- **You are in the season where you are for a purpose!**

- What others do to hurt you, turns out to be for your good is what makes the difference!

- **Each life's experience teaches you something!**

- Rely on good memories, to help you make it through the rough times of your sentence!

- The only person you can truly trust is you and God!

- **Trust and obey God's word while sitting in your pod!**

- Keep hope alive while on your journey!

- You are who you are, inside or outside confined walls through your memory!

- Each person has a unique gift, help others find their gift!

- After a rain, the sun comes out and a beautiful rainbow appears, look up and see the lift.

- **Don't ruin the present worrying about how the past will affect your future.**

- Because yesterday ended last night, and your future is a new beginning.

- **"Persistence will get you there: Consistency will keep you there, and** nothing else in the world can take the place of that; Talent will not; Genius will not, Education will not.

- Be steadfast, unmovable always pushing forward into your destiny. **BE RESILIENT!**

- Don't be afraid to jump into the deep. Jesus walked on water, he can and will save you!

- When someone tells you don't say anything, DON'T SAY ANYTHING! KEEPING MY MOUTH SHUT WAS A PRICELESS LESSON LEARNED... and now to continue in this as I'm on the outside and moving forward.

- The less said the better.... Less is more.

Although the scriptures are the perfect end all, be all, to me, the complete and solid foundation to everything I believe; I'd like to close the end of this book on an exceptional note. There is a friend who is like a brother to me, TAHEIM NIPPER. He is an author, poet, father and an awesome husband to his precious wife, Pastor Colleen Nipper, Total Praise Worship Center on County Line Road in Atlanta, Georgia. Tahiem wrote a poem called **_Transcendence_** I'd like to share. It speaks to my experience and I feel it's a POWERFUL way to close my story.

"Transcendence"

Tried to disgrace me with cuffs, wrap me in fetters, bind me with chains

Thought I'd have my day in court, but the motion was sustained

Confined to a place and a space which is less than humane

But they didn't count on my Maker, who made me with a purpose,

Fashioned me in the womb, and set me apart before I even *HAD* a given name

Even with reading glasses, a rocking chair, and a spot of tea, you STILL wouldn't believe my story

From the charges, to the arrest, to the jumpsuit, it was **ALL** handled poorly

And to put a nice little "bow" on things; they left me to rot in this earthly version of purgatory

What they didn't count on though, even in the midst of . . . was me giving GOD all the Glory!

I don't look like what I been through

Been to the mountain top, which was flipped on its ear, twisted 180°, and left my name imbrued

Many are called but chosen, are few

Even if the process itself has me vexed, He's gon BUST that yoke on my neck, ordering my steps, while *He* creates something new

If they could net profit from my pain, they would've surely charged admission

They made conscious decisions to assassinate my character with insidious derision

But as always God had the vision, for me to gather, galvanize and lead these women

Like Joseph in the pit, Daniel in The Den, I'd **also** been commissioned to ***prosper*** in prison

I remembered who I was in Him

Didn't concern myself with Tanika, Shaniqua, nor Kim

Just stayed in my Word, and hit the gym

I was made in my Father's image, there was no NEED to try and fit in

The devil tried to come at me with 2-guns blazin'

But I'm my Fathers child, **that's** why I'm worth savin'

I'll always remember to whom I belong, recalling the moment that I surrendered, and gave in

Praising Him in song at the top of my lungs, while singin' *"You're Amazin'"*!"

2017 was an extraordinarily challenging year, one of the most difficult by far

You too have experienced the subpar, things so intolerable you wish you had an avatar

Sometimes you have to encourage your**self**, so in times like these I remember: I was **born** a star

So, if you're sitting, standing or laying reading on in agreement, you should praise Him . . . right where you are!

I clearly do not know everything, but I'll enlighten you when, and if, I can

Just like there's an 'App' for everything, for every living organism, He has a plan

He doesn't have to hit the game-winning shot or have Billboard 100 hits for me to be a fan

I'm sold because he has delivered me, He is the 1st AND the last, He is **that** great . . . I AM!

"In closing" as some of us preachers say when we're closing our message to the congregation, yes, you sent me to prison. You took away my privileges, my clothes, my name, my identity and the time I lost from doing what I "wanted" to do. However, I believe God used that time to prepare me for what "He" has for me to do. You shackled my hands and feet. However, you could not lock up my belief in God, His word, and my ministry of the gospel of Jesus Christ. Purpose prevailed!

"To God be the glory for the things he has done!"

I was Imprisoned, But Not Bound... AMEN

ACKNOWLEDGEMENTS

I'd like to acknowledge those who have helped me along the way throughout life and although they are gone on, they will never be forgotten and I want the world to know how much they were so very much appreciated. I could not attend the funeral because I was in the custody of Department of corrections, there would have been no other reason I would not have been there.

Rebecca Lynn White, my dear friend and prayer partner for a number of years. Becky, I cannot even find words to express how much I miss you. Tears still flood my eyes just to think of you.   Raymond and Rai'Jene please know that she was a precious jewel to me, a diamond that will forever shine in my mind, heart and spirit. Becky, I know I will see you again on the other side. **April 2, 2018**

William Clifford Voyles, who I fondly called dad. He was better to me than my own father. Not just because he loaned me the money to purchase my second property, but he gave me away at my wedding to John Gude. He had been a dad to me for over 15 years. Dad I love you dearly. You will be forever missed and remembered in my heart. **October 17, 2017**

Marie Garrett, a woman who mentored me in the church during my young adult years, Pinewood Tabernacle in Toledo Ohio for almost 20 years. Your ministry is what I called basic training. I still quote so much that I learned from you. You were a part of the solid foundation that has upheld me for all these years. Never forgotten, and forever loved. **August 2, 2016**

Pastor Randy Dean Hall, a prophet, pastor, and just plain ole Brother Randy as he preferred to be called. You instilled so much faith and resilience in me with the bible teachings you stood on for more than the 15 years that I was a part of your ministry. *Because of you*, I am the women of faith that I am today. You will forever be a thread in the fabric of my ministry. I just believe you are sitting at the right hand of the father and that's the only thing that comforts me of your absence from this earth today. You are forever in my HALL OF FAME!

THANK YOU ALL FROM THE CENTER OF MY HEART.

1. **Pastor John Bailey**, GOSPEL NATIONS CHRISTIAN FELLOWSHIP of Powder Springs Georgia. Thank you for not only employing Travis as your organist, but for being a beacon of light with teachings of the unadulterated truth in the word of God. I appreciate you preforming the eulogy of his home going to be with the Lord Thank you church family

2. **Pastor Hosea Clay**, NEW LIFE FELLOWSHIP for being Travis's friend. He valued your friendship.

3. **Pastor Victor Walker**, CREATED LIGHT MINISTRY, thank you for allowing God to use you in his last days to minister to his soul and allowing him to express his feelings and expressions of his love for God in your church just days before his passing.

4. **Pastor Kenneth Cudjoe**,- THE WAY OF LIFE MINISTRY ...thank you for EVERYTHING

5. **Pastor Kenneth Johnson**,- THE BREAKING RELIGION MOVEMENT – You are SO awesome

6. **Minister Lucille Searcy, Minister Shannon Lucas,** thank you all for your powerful anointed participation in the service.

7. **Pastor Dantzler**; The proclamation will be framed and will hang in my home with Travis pictures.

8. **Delshonda Lucas**, thank you for allowing the Lord to have you pick and purchase Travis's entire home going attire for his last day on earth.

9. To my immediate family and church members, and employees, how can I thank you for all that you have done for me? You comforted and stood by me when I needed you most.

Every minister who read scripture, spoke from your experiences with Travis, played music with him, or allowed him to play in your church, Thank You.
Music was near and dear to his heart.

Everyone who sent flowers, cards, telegrams, gave money, spoke words of encouragement, and all of you that participated in making the home going service bearable for me, I thank you so very much.

If I have left anyone out by name, please forgive me and know that you are as special as anyone named. The many who attended from far and near; Ohio, Texas, California, Alabama, North Carolina and Georgia. **AND** the hundreds of you who could not attend but sent your love, support and prayers, please know that I am grateful and appreciative of everything you have done. Your thoughtfulness will never be forgotten. You are unconditionally loved.

IF I COULD NAME THE SUN AND THE MOON, THEY WOULD BE CALLED BOB AND JANIS.... YOU HAVE BEEN SUCH A FRIEND IN DEED; YOUR EXTENDED EXPRESSION OF LOVE, AS A VERY EXTRODINARY HELP IN MY TIME OF NEED....LEAVES ME IN AWE.

YOUR INVESTMENT OF TRUST IN ME HAS BEEN REMARKABLE.

I WILL ALWAYS BE AVAILABLE TO YOU, AND OUR FAVORITE PERSON, THE TRUST AND SUPPORT YOU CONTINUE TO SHOW WILL NEVER BE FORGOTTEN.

I CANNOT SAY THANK YOU ENOUGH.

ABOUT THE AUTHOR
Edith M. Page, RN

Edith attended Michael J. Owens College, The University of Toledo and Medical College of Ohio. She became a professional Registered Nurse in 1988. She went on to receive a full scholarship to study and earned a certification in Gerontology at Kennesaw State University in 2015. Edith received training in Business and Ministry from the Bronner Business Institute and The Women's Institute of Ministry. She is currently completing a degree in legal studies in pursuit of receiving a Juris doctorate from Law School.

Edith is the Business founder of The Top of Line Residential Care and Development, Inc. where she passionately served the mentally challenged in homes that she operated in Powder Springs Georgia, for almost twenty years.

She was a member of Sword of the Lord International Ministries for 15 years where the Late Pastor Randy D. Hall was her Pastor. She is currently a member of Word of Faith Family Worship Cathedral in Austell Georgia, where Bishop Dale C. Bronner is the Founder and Pastor. Edith is a bible scholar who loves God with her whole heart.

Edith was born in Toledo Ohio to Spencer and Merlinda Page on January 7, 1960. Edith has two Sisters Gwen and Cynthia and two brothers, Timothy and James where we love and support one another in every way we know how. Living with her devoted and supportive husband Mr. Osvaldo Hernandez. Edith continues in the faith trusting God for a future that will fulfil her purpose in life, as she continues to serve her heavenly father, **Jehovah.**

Edith and Osvaldo Hernandez

REFERENCES

Quotes, and Sayings - From Bishop Dale C. Bronner Sermons: (Over a period of 8 years). Senior Pastor, Word of Faith Family Worship Cathedral, Austell Georgia

Sharon and David Beaner - Overcoming Adversities, Seeds of Love Ministry

King James Bible - Thompson-Chain-Reference

Poem - Transcendence written by Tahiem Nipper

Songs - Lauren Dangle, Jekalyn Carr, Smokie Norful,

Poem - Tim Nym's - Pray Until You Get Your Sugar, written by Timothy Wynn Page

Quote - Carrie Underwood's Book, Cry Pretty

The Creed - Emanuel Women's Facility

BOOK ORDER FORM IMPRISONED, BUT NOT BOUND

Edith M. Page
4960 Brownville Road
Powder Springs, Georgia 30127

E-Mail Address: edithpage7@gmail.com

YOUR SHIPPING INFORMATION

Name: _____

Address: _____

Phone Number: _____

E-Mail Address: _____

For Every Book Sold Via This Book Order Form, $5.00 Will Be Donated To Prison Inmates and Their Families in Honor of Dr. Jamila Hammon.

Price Per Book - $19.99 (Check or Money Order)

If Mailed, Include $5.01 For Postage

Number of Books Ordered:_____

I've saved the best for last.... **MY BABY SISTER CYNTHIA.**